First World War
and Army of Occupation
War Diary
France, Belgium and Germany

62 DIVISION
186 Infantry Brigade
Duke of Wellington's (West Riding Regiment)
2/5th Battalion
9 October 1914 - 31 January 1918

WO95/3086/2

The Naval & Military Press Ltd
www.nmarchive.com
Published in association with The National Archives

Published by

The Naval & Military Press Ltd

Unit 10 Ridgewood Industrial Park,

Uckfield, East Sussex,

TN22 5QE England

Tel: +44 (0) 1825 749494

www.naval-military-press.com

www.nmarchive.com

This diary has been reprinted in facsimile from the original. Any imperfections are inevitably reproduced and the quality may fall short of modern type and cartographic standards.

© Crown Copyright

Images reproduced by permission of The National Archives, London, England, 2015.

Contents

Document type	Place/Title	Date From	Date To
Heading	WO95/3086/2		
Heading	62 Div 186 Bde 2/5 Duke Of Wellington W Riding Regt 1914 Sep-1918 Jan		
Heading	War Diary of The 2/5th Battalion West Riding Regt From 9/10/1914 To 06.1.17		
War Diary	Huddersfield	09/10/1914	02/03/1915
War Diary	Derby	02/03/1915	16/03/1915
War Diary	Huddersfield And Derby	01/02/1915	25/03/1915
War Diary	Doncaster	14/04/1915	18/05/1915
War Diary	Thoresby	28/06/1915	07/08/1915
War Diary	Babworth	14/08/1915	14/10/1915
War Diary	Gainsborough	16/10/1915	24/11/1915
War Diary	Nerve Castle-On-Sykes	30/11/1915	06/01/1916
War Diary	Larkhill	16/01/1916	10/06/1916
War Diary	Henham	14/06/1916	03/11/1916
War Diary	Bedford	06/01/1917	06/01/1917
Miscellaneous	West Riding Regiment		
Miscellaneous	O.C. 2/5 Th. Battn Duke of Wellingtons Rgt	19/03/1916	19/03/1916
Miscellaneous	O.C. 2/5 B.Of W.Regt	20/03/1916	20/03/1916
Heading	War Diary of 2/5th Battalion Duke Of Wellingtons Regt From Jany 10th 1917 To Jany 31st 1917		
War Diary	Bedford	10/01/1917	10/01/1917
War Diary	Southampton	10/01/1917	11/01/1917
War Diary	Le Havre	12/01/1917	13/01/1917
War Diary	Auxi-Le-Chateau	14/01/1917	14/01/1917
War Diary	Noeux	22/01/1917	22/01/1917
War Diary	Amplier	22/01/1917	23/01/1917
War Diary	Bus-Les-Artois	23/01/1917	31/01/1917
Heading	War Diary of 2/5 Bn Duke of Wellingtons Regt. From 1st Feb 1917 To 28th Feby 1917 Volume II		
War Diary	War Diary of 2/5 Bn Duke of Wellingtons Regt. From 1st Feb 1917 To 28th Feby 1917 Volume II		
War Diary	Bus	07/02/1917	13/02/1917
War Diary	Beaumont Hamel	17/02/1917	17/02/1917
War Diary	Mailly-Maillet	18/02/1917	22/02/1917
War Diary	Mailly-Woods East	22/02/1917	25/02/1917
War Diary	Beaumont Hamel	26/02/1917	26/02/1917
War Diary	Wundtwerk	27/02/1917	28/02/1917
Miscellaneous	2/5th Bn. Duke Of Wellington's Regiment.	04/02/1917	04/02/1917
Heading	War Diary Of 2/5 Bn Duke Of Wellingtons Regt Volume III March 1917		
War Diary	Wundtwerk	01/03/1917	01/03/1917
War Diary	Engelbelmer	01/03/1917	08/03/1917
War Diary	Pelican Camp	09/03/1917	15/03/1917
War Diary	Miraumont	16/03/1917	17/03/1917
War Diary	Achiet Le Petit	17/03/1917	23/03/1917
War Diary	Gomiecourt	31/03/1917	31/03/1917
War Diary	Behagnies	02/04/1917	02/04/1917
Heading	War Diary 2/5 Bn Duke of Wellingtons Regt. Volume IV April 1st-April 30th 1917		

War Diary	Behagnies	01/04/1917	11/04/1917
War Diary	Mory	13/04/1917	02/05/1917
Miscellaneous	Appendix A.	02/04/1914	02/04/1914
Miscellaneous	Appendix B Honours and Rewards		
War Diary	Appendix B Honours and Rewards		
Heading	War Diary 2/5th Bn Duke Of Wellingtons Regt May 1st 1917 To May 31st 1917 Volume 5		
War Diary	Mory	01/05/1917	02/05/1917
War Diary	Ecoust	03/05/1917	04/05/1917
War Diary	Mory Copse	05/05/1917	07/05/1917
War Diary	Ervillers	08/05/1917	13/05/1917
War Diary	Ecoust	14/05/1917	20/05/1917
War Diary	Courcelles	21/05/1917	29/05/1917
War Diary	Achiet Le Petit	30/05/1917	31/05/1917
Heading	2/5th Battalion Duke Of Wellingtons Regiment War Diary June 1st To June 30th 1917 Volume 6		
War Diary	Achite Le Petit	01/06/1917	26/06/1917
War Diary	Vaulx	27/06/1917	27/06/1917
War Diary	In The Line	28/06/1917	30/06/1917
Heading	War Diary 2/5th Bn. Duke Of Wellington's Regiment July 1917 Volume 7		
War Diary	Noreuil	01/07/1917	05/07/1917
War Diary	Beugnatre	06/07/1917	13/07/1917
War Diary	Lagnicourt	14/07/1917	21/07/1917
War Diary	Vaulx	22/07/1917	25/07/1917
War Diary	Lagnicourt	26/07/1917	29/07/1917
War Diary	Beugnatre	30/07/1917	31/07/1917
Heading	War Diary Of 2/5th Bn. Duke Of Wellington's Rgt Period 1st To 31st August 1917 Volume VIII		
War Diary	Beugnatre	01/08/1917	08/08/1917
War Diary	Noreuil	05/08/1917	13/08/1917
War Diary	Beugnatre	14/08/1917	20/08/1917
War Diary	Bullecourt	21/08/1917	28/08/1917
War Diary	Mory	29/08/1917	31/08/1917
Heading	War Diary of 2/5th Bn. Duke of Wellington's Regiment From 1st September 1917 To 30th September 1917 Volume 9		
War Diary	Mory	01/09/1917	05/09/1917
War Diary	Beugnatre	06/09/1917	12/09/1917
War Diary	Noreiul	13/09/1917	29/09/1917
War Diary	Beugnatre	30/09/1917	30/09/1917
Heading	War Diary of 2/5th Bn. Duke of Wellingtons Regiment From 1st October 1917 To 31st October 1917 Volume 10		
War Diary	Beugnatre	01/10/1917	07/10/1917
War Diary	Noreuil	08/10/1917	10/10/1917
War Diary	Beugnatre	11/10/1917	12/10/1917
War Diary	Beulencourt	13/10/1917	30/10/1917
War Diary	Courcelles	31/10/1917	31/10/1917
Heading	War Diary of 2/5th Bn. Duke of Wellingtons Regt From 1st November 1917 To 30th November 1917 Vol 11		
War Diary	Gouy	01/11/1917	13/11/1917
War Diary	Achiet Le Petit	14/11/1917	16/11/1917
War Diary	Lechelle	17/11/1917	18/11/1917
War Diary	Bertincourt	19/11/1917	20/11/1917
War Diary	Kangaroo Alley N W Graincourt	21/11/1917	21/11/1917

War Diary	Hindenburg Line K.16.b	22/11/1917	22/11/1917
War Diary	Havrincourt Wood	23/11/1917	23/11/1917
War Diary	Bertincourt	24/11/1917	25/11/1917
War Diary	Sunken Rd N.W. Anneux	26/11/1917	26/11/1917
War Diary	Bourlon Wood	27/11/1917	28/11/1917
War Diary	Hindenburg Line K9c	29/11/1917	30/11/1917
Miscellaneous	2/5th. Bn. Duke Of Wellington's Regiment.	17/11/1917	17/11/1917
Miscellaneous	2/5th. Bn. Duke Of Wellington's Regiment.	21/11/1917	21/11/1917
Miscellaneous	2/5th. Bn. Duke Of Wellington's Regiment.	26/11/1917	26/11/1917
Heading	War Diary of 2/5th Bn. Duke of Wellington's Regt From 1st Dec 1917 To 31st Dec 1917 Volume 12		
War Diary	Hindenburg Line KaD	01/12/1917	01/12/1917
War Diary	Hindenburg Line K.2.b.1.3.a	02/12/1917	03/12/1917
War Diary	Lebucquiere	04/12/1917	04/12/1917
War Diary	Bellacourt	05/12/1917	05/12/1917
War Diary	Bailleul Aux Cornailles	07/12/1917	10/12/1917
War Diary	Annezin	11/12/1917	14/12/1917
War Diary	Cantraine	15/12/1917	18/12/1917
War Diary	Annezin	19/12/1917	19/12/1917
War Diary	Bailleul	20/12/1917	31/12/1917
Heading	War Diary of 2/5th Bn. Duke of Wellingtons Regt. From January 1st 1918 To January 31st 1918 Volume 13		
Heading	War Diary of 2/5th Duke of Wellingtons Rgt. From January 1st-1918 To January 31st-1918 Volume 13		
War Diary	Bailleul	01/01/1918	09/01/1918
War Diary	St. Aubin	10/01/1918	14/01/1918
War Diary	Oppy	15/01/1918	22/01/1918
War Diary	St Aubin	23/01/1918	31/01/1918
Map	Map		
Map	Beauvais		
Miscellaneous	Beauvais 21		

mom 5506/3086(2)

mom 5505/3086(2)

62 DIV

186 BDE

2/5 DUKE OF WELLINGTON W RIDING REGT

1914 SEP — 1918 JAN

Absorbed by 5 BN

Confidential:—

WAR DIARY

of the

2/5th Battalion West Riding Regt

From 9/10/1914 To 20/8/1915

Army Form C. 2118.

WAR DIARY
or
INTELLIGENCE SUMMARY.
(Erase heading not required.)

Instructions regarding War Diaries and Intelligence Summaries are contained in F. S. Regs., Part II. and the Staff Manual respectively. Title pages will be prepared in manuscript.

Place	Date	Hour	Summary of Events and Information	Remarks and references to Appendices
Huddersfield	9.10.14	—	5th (Reserve) Battalion, Duke of Wellington's West Riding Regiment was formed under the command of Lieut. Col. w. Brooke V.D. with Head Quarters at the Drill Hall Huddersfield, and 98 N.C.Os and men were transferred from the 5th Battalion then stationed at Selby lines to form the nucleus of the new Battalion. The Battalion was recruited in Huddersfield and district and soon	
	11.1.15		to supply drafts to the 5th Battalion. First Draft of 193 men sent to the 5th Battalion then stationed at Doncaster.	
	1.2.15		Line Officers, namely 2nd Lieuts. A McIntosh, M. Jost, P.H. Kaye, H. Kippan & E.C.R. Laycock sent to the 5th Battalion at Doncaster during this period.	
	4.1.15		The Battalion received orders to mount a guard of 3 N.C.Os & 33 men at the works of Messrs Read Holliday & Sons Ltd, Huddersfield, on deck and the Guard was continued till relieved by the N.R. on the 13.3.15.	

WAR DIARY or INTELLIGENCE SUMMARY

Army Form C. 2118.

(Erase heading not required.)

Instructions regarding War Diaries and Intelligence Summaries are contained in F. S. Regs., Part II. and the Staff Manual respectively. Title pages will be prepared in manuscript.

Place	Date	Hour	Summary of Events and Information	Remarks and references to Appendices
Huddersfield	6.2.15	—	Battalion known as 2/5th Battalion Duke of Wellington's West Riding Regiment from this date.	W.D.
			During this period 240 men under 19 years of age & rejected men on medical grounds were transferred to the 5th Battalion	W.D.
	22.2.15	—	Third draft of 30 men sent to the 5th Battalion at Doncaster	W.D.
	2.3.15		The Battalion proceeded to Doity 803 strong exclusive of Officers & was billeted in private houses in the Normanton Ward	W.D.
Doity	2.3.15		The Battalion was now under the command of the O.C. 2nd/2nd West Riding Infantry Brigade. Brigadier General Deaby	W.D.
			6th Draft of 30 men sent to the 5th Battalion at Doncaster	W.D.
Huddersfield	1.3.15		7th and 8th Drafts consisting of 24, 6, 26 and 13 men sent to 5th Battalion at Doncaster	W.D.
Doity	25.3.15		10, 24, 6, 26 and 13 men sent to 5th Battalion at Doncaster	W.D.
Doity	3.4.15		The Battalion received orders to mount a Guard of 2 Officers, 5 N.C.O.s and 43 men over the magazine at Selby & this Guard was continued till relieved by another Regiment on the 6.5.15.	W.D.
"	12.4.15		The Battalion proceeded by rail to Doncaster and went under canvas	W.D.

Army Form C. 2118.

WAR DIARY
or
INTELLIGENCE SUMMARY.
(Erase heading not required.)

Instructions regarding War Diaries and Intelligence Summaries are contained in F.S. Regs., Part II. and the Staff Manual respectively. Title pages will be prepared in manuscript.

Place	Date	Hour	Summary of Events and Information	Remarks and references to Appendices
Doncaster	14.4.15		on the Race Course Doncaster. Draft of 99 N.C.Os and men transferred to this Battalion from the 5th Battalion.	
"	13.5.15		Home Service men transferred to 26th Provisional Battalion for home defence only.	
"	16.5.15		Japanese Rifles issued to this Battalion	
"	18.5.15		5th Battalion proceeded by road to Thoresby Park. Roll: 839 strong & went under canvas.	
Thoresby	28.6.15		Ninth Draft of 99 N.C.Os & men sent abroad to join the 5th Battalion serving with the Expeditionary Forces in France	
"	4.7.15		3 Officers sent to the 5th Battalion serving in France with the Expeditionary Force, namely, 2nd Lieuts: C.E. Sutcliffe, A.N. Sharpe and J.H. Ward.	
"	17.7.15		All C.L.L.E. rifles withdrawn from the Battalion	
"	78.15		The Battalion proceeded by road to Babworth, Retford to camp under canvas.	

Army Form C. 2118.

WAR DIARY
— or —
INTELLIGENCE SUMMARY.
(Erase heading not required.)

Instructions regarding War Diaries and Intelligence Summaries are contained in F.S. Regs., Part II. and the Staff Manual respectively. Title pages will be prepared in manuscript.

Place	Date	Hour	Summary of Events and Information	Remarks and references to Appendices
Bulwark Thursday	14.8.15	—	Draft of 41 N.C.Os and men sent to the 5th Battalion serving abroad with the Expeditionary Forces in France	
Bulwark	16.8.15		Lieut.Col. W. COOPER. V.D. transferred to the 26th Provisional Battalion and Major J.L. ROBINSON assumed Company Command.	
do.	10.9.15		Lieut. George B. Houlden seconded, dated 13th April 1915.	
do.	11.9.15		Lieut. W.C. Thornton resigned his Commission owing to ill health 10.9.15.	
do.	do.		Captain G.E. Bedfirth appointed Adjutant of the 2/5th Battalion West Riding Regiment as from 20.7.15.	
do.	12.7.15		2nd Lieut. Thomas W. M. Mellow taken on the strength of the Battalion as from 10.7.15. (additional)	
do.	12.9.15		2nd Lieut. M. Howarth and 2nd Lieut. E. Bond transferred from the 1/7 West Riding Regiment and taken on the strength of the Battalion from 5.8.15	
do.	12.9.15		2nd Lieut. A.D. Broadbent transferred to the 5th Battalion serving in France with the British Expeditionary Force 20.9.15.	
do.	12.9.15		2nd Lieut. G.R. Gledhill transferred to the 5th Battalion serving in France with the British Expeditionary Force 21.9.15.	

Army Form C. 2118.

WAR DIARY
INTELLIGENCE SUMMARY
(Erase heading not required.)

Place	Date	Hour	Summary of Events and Information	Remarks and references to Appendices
Harworth	24.9.15		Colonel W.O.M. Moss assumed command of the Battalion 24.9.15. 2nd Lieut. D.H.H. Jackson and 2nd Lieut. E.G. Workinson transferred to the 5th Battalion serving in France with the British Expeditionary Force 30.9.15.	
do	1.10.15			
do	18.10.15		The Battalion proceeded by road from Bodworth to Gainsborough to go into winter quarters there which consisted of public buildings, an auction room and "Morton House", a large private house.	
Gainsborough	16.10.15		2nd Lieut. J.G. Walker, 2nd Lieut. J.B. Cockhill, 2nd Lieut. L.D. Goodall and 2nd Lieut. C. Bond transferred to 5th Battalion serving with the British Expeditionary Force in France.	
do	19.10.15		Lieut. C.W.D. Harpe resigned his Commission on account of ill health 15.10.15.	
do	1.11.15		2nd Lieut. S. to Lyffer, 2nd Lieut. E.D. Ay and 2nd Lieut B.W. Rounder transferred to the 5th Battalion serving in France with the British Expeditionary Force.	
do	24.11.15		The Battalion proceeded by train from Gainsborough to Newcastle-on-Tyne and went into quarters there in public buildings.	

WAR DIARY
INTELLIGENCE SUMMARY

Army Form C. 2118.

Place	Date	Hour	Summary of Events and Information	Remarks and references to Appendices
Newcastle-on-Tyne	30.11.15		Lieut: R. M. Parker, 2nd Lieut: E. Y. Sykes, 2nd Lieut: J. C. H. Ambler and 2nd Lieut: J. W. M. Sutton transferred to the 5th Battalion (serving in France) with the British Expeditionary Force.	4/y
do.	8.12.15.		2nd Lieut: Tom C. Jacob, 2nd Lieut: William L. Thomas and 2nd Lieut: Hans G. Hodgkinson transferred to this Battalion from 11th Battalion West Riding Regiment.	4/y
do.	28.12.15.		Lieut: D. C. Lyall transferred to the 5th Battalion West Riding Regiment serving with the British Expeditionary Force in France.	4/y
do.	6.1.16		The Battalion proceeded by rail from Newcastle on Tyne to Brocton Station and went into huts in No. 2 A Camp, Cannock Chase, Rawhill, Staffordshire.	4/y
Rawhill	16.1.16		The Battalion moved from No. 2 A Camp to No. 5 Camp Rawhill.	4/y
do.	18.1.16		Captain C. B. Harris (Shropshire Light Infantry) attached to the Battalion for duty and taken on its strength.	4/y
do.	20.1.16		Captain W. Lawson having been demobilised in pursuit of the strength of the Battalion as from 29.12.15. Employers Messrs Abbey & Lawson Lieb. Sheffield.	4/y
do.	20.1.16		Lieut: E. J. Lovelick (2nd Battalion West Riding Regiment) attached to this	4/y

6.

WAR DIARY
—or—
INTELLIGENCE SUMMARY.
(Erase heading not required.)

Army Form C. 2118.

Place	Date	Hour	Summary of Events and Information	Remarks and references to Appendices
Larkhill	24.1.16		Battalion for duty. Lieut. Y. Garay (1st Battalion Norfolk Regiment) attached to this Battalion for duty as from 23.1.16	
do	29.1.16		2nd Lieut. J.M. Kenton (2nd Battalion Royal Munster Fusiliers) attached to this Battalion for duty.	
do	30.1.16		Draft of 23 men transferred from the 3/5th Battalion West Riding Regiment to this Battalion and taken on the strength.	
do	30.1.16		Captain P. Thomson having been transferred to the 26th Provisional Battalion is struck off the strength of this Battalion.	
do	5.2.16		Captain R.C.R. and 2nd Lieut. W.A. Gorfour transferred to the 26th Provisional Battalion, both having been seconded for duty with that Battalion.	
do	5.2.16		2nd Lieut. J.H. Harrison rejoined the 11th West Riding Regiment	
do	14.2.16		2nd Lieut. J.M. Kenton (2nd Battalion Royal Munster Fusiliers) having rejoined his Regiment is struck off the strength of this Battalion.	
do	19.2.16		Draft of 14 men transferred from the 3/5th Battalion West Riding Regiment and taken on the strength of this Battalion.	

Army Form C. 2118.

WAR DIARY
or
INTELLIGENCE SUMMARY.
(Erase heading not required.)

Instructions regarding War Diaries and Intelligence Summaries are contained in F.S. Regs., Part II. and the Staff Manual respectively. Title pages will be prepared in manuscript.

Place	Date	Hour	Summary of Events and Information	Remarks and references to Appendices
Larkhill	23.2.16	—	2nd Lieut. N.S. Dowdy transferred to the 26th Provisional Battalion and struck off the strength of this Battalion.	A/y
do.	1.3.16	—	2nd Lieut. J.P. Turner (3rd Warwickshire Regiment) attached to this Battalion for duty 29.2.16.	A/y
do.	1.3.16	—	2nd Lieut. A.R. Bonsfield (2nd East Surrey Regiment) attached to this Battalion for duty.	A/y
do.	9.3.16	—	Percy Coxley Desmond appointed Quartermaster to this Battalion with the honorary rank of Lieutenant dated 1.1.16.	A/y
do.	9.3.16 to 31.3.16	—	Drafts of men numbering 614 in total joined Headquarters and were taken on the strength of the Battalion on and between these dates.	A/y
Larkhill	14.3.16	—	Captain C.D. Harris, King's Shropshire Light Infantry having been ordered to join the Expeditionary Force is struck off the strength of the Battalion.	A/y
do.	20.3.16	—	Major J.L. Robinson having been transferred to the Territorial Force Reserve is struck off the strength of the Battalion from 13.3.16.	A/y
do.	22.3.16	—	Lieut. Y.G. Garland, 2nd Lieut. Y.C. Jacobs and 2nd Lieut. A.G. Hodgkinson having been transferred from the 3rd Line are taken on the strength of this Battalion.	A/y
do.	24.3.16	—	2nd Lieut. W.M. Fisher and 2nd Lieut. A.H. Oldham taken on the strength of the Battalion 23.3.16.	A/y

WAR DIARY
INTELLIGENCE SUMMARY.
(Erase heading not required.)

Army Form C. 2118.

Instructions regarding War Diaries and Intelligence Summaries are contained in F.S. Regs., Part II. and the Staff Manual respectively. Title pages will be prepared in manuscript.

Place	Date	Hour	Summary of Events and Information	Remarks and references to Appendices
Lichfield	6.4.16	—	2nd Lieutenant Butterworth F.W. taken on the strength of the Battalion 5.4.16	
do.	13.4.16	—	2nd Lieut: Goldeller L.P. transferred from the 11th West Riding Regiment with precedence on from 10.4.15 dated 9.4.16.	
do.	14.4.16	—	Major J.A.D. Best, Royal Inniskilling Fusiliers assumed command of the Battalion 14.4.16.	
do.	20.4.16	—	Colonel W.O.M. Mase having relinquished command of the Battalion is struck off the strength from 16.4.16.	
do.	25.4.16	—	2nd Lieut: Ayrton D.A. taken on the strength of the Battalion 22.4.16.	
do.	28.4.16	—	2nd Lieut: N.E. Bentley and 2nd Lieut: H.A. Simmonds having been transferred from the 3/5th Battalion are taken on the strength of this Battalion from 24.4.16.	
do.	29.4.16	—	Major R.E. Rogers, North Staffordshire Regiment, having reported for duty on April 25th is taken on the strength from that date and takes over the duties of second in command.	
do.	5.5.16	—	Major (temporary Lieutenant Colonel) J.A.D. Best, Royal Inniskilling Fusiliers to be a Companion of the "Distinguished Service Order" dated 2.5.16.	
do.	9.5.16 and 10.6.16	—	Major Thomas A.D. Best promoted Lieutenant Colonel (temporary) 14 April 1916. The Battalion proceeded by rail from Amesbury to Mullacrough and went into Camp	

WAR DIARY

INTELLIGENCE SUMMARY.

(Erase heading not required.)

Army Form C. 2118.

Place	Date	Hour	Summary of Events and Information	Remarks and references to Appendices
Hurdcott	4.6.16	—	ends camp in Hurdcott Park near Wingford Suffolk. 2nd Lieut: G.D. Bishop, 3/9th Battalion Middlesex Regiment attached to this Battalion	4/3
do.	29.6.16	—	Lieut G. Garvey having joined the 1st Garrison Battalion East Kent Regiment is struck off the strength of this Battalion from 23.6.16	4/4
do.	10.7.16	—	Captain E.C.B. Knapp and Captain G.M.M. Miller 10th Battalion Royal Scots (Ryl.Scots) Corps taken on the strength of this Battalion. 2nd Lieut: W.A. Bowser of the 3/9th Battalion Middlesex Regiment taken on the strength of this Battalion.	4/5
			2nd Lieut: J.F. Younia and 2nd Lieut: H. Bousfield having rejoined their units are struck off the strength of this Battalion	4/6
do.	11.7.16	—	2nd Lieut: D. Wilson struck off the strength of this Battalion and rejoined the 3/6th Battalion Duke of Wellington's Regiment.	4/7
do.	12.7.16	—	Lieut: B.J.V. Bartlett having been transferred to the Royal Flying Corps is struck off the strength of this Battalion.	4/8
do.	24.7.16	—	2nd Lieut: J.J. Walters of the Northern Cyclist Battalion having been posted to this Battalion for duty is taken on the strength from 22.7.16	4/9

10.

Army Form C. 2118.

WAR DIARY
or
INTELLIGENCE SUMMARY.
(Erase heading not required.)

Instructions regarding War Diaries and Intelligence Summaries are contained in F. S. Regs., Part II. and the Staff Manual respectively. Title pages will be prepared in manuscript.

Place	Date	Hour	Summary of Events and Information	Remarks and references to Appendices
Horbury	24.7.16	—	Lieut. A. M. Balfour, 1st Monston Cyclist Battalion, having been posted to this Battalion for duty is taken on the strength from this date	1/4
do.	26.7.16	—	Lieut. P. R. Kelley, 1st Northern Cyclist Battalion having been posted to this Battalion for duty is taken on the strength from this date	2/4
do.	26.7.16	—	Battalion with the Ramsgate Scouts from Huddersfield proceeded by road to the entrance gates to Walshingham Hall, Walshingham, near Reeves and there mounted guard. His majesty King George V, in column of route afterwards the troops lined the roadway and His majesty drove past in his Motor Car	3/4
Horbury	2.8.16 / 3.8.16	—	Air Raid warning received & of the Battalion was doing night Outpost duties on the Milborough Common. Zeppelin heard overhead but could not be seen on account of mist	4/4
do.	1.9.16 ? 3.8.16	—	Air Raid warning received and Battalion went out of Camp into woods east of Camp. Zeppelin passed right over, going in an easterly direction and to see between 12.30 and 1 am and dropped bombs in Hilmer Covert and on the foreshore 1½ miles N of Southwold	5/4
do.	3.8.16	—	Capt. E. C. P. Swoop transferred to 2/6th Battalion Duke of Wellington's Regiment.	6/4
			Capt. G. W. M. Miller transferred to 2/4th Battalion Duke of Wellington's Regiment	7/4
			Lieut. R. C. M. Leather transferred from 2/6th Battalion Duke of Wellington's Regiment to this	8/4

11.

WAR DIARY
INTELLIGENCE SUMMARY
(Erase heading not required.)

Army Form C. 2118.

Instructions regarding War Diaries and Intelligence Summaries are contained in F. S. Regs., Part II. and the Staff Manual respectively. Title pages will be prepared in manuscript.

Place	Date	Hour	Summary of Events and Information	Remarks and references to Appendices
Henlow	13.8.16	—	Battalion not taken in the strength	
Henlow	18.8.16	—	Lieut. K.W. Caldecott transferred from 2/16th Battalion Duke of Wellingtons regiment to King's Battalion and taken on the strength.	
Henlow	2.9.16	—	Zeppelin clearly visible passed over the Camp going inland in a westerly direction about 9.50 pm. A Zeppelin was brought down burned and crashed at the village of Cuffley near Enfield later the same night.	
Henlow	22.9.16	—	Zeppelin clearly visible passed over the camp about 9.30 pm going inland in a westerly direction. Two Zeppelins were brought down later the same night in the County of Essex, one burned and wrecked the other only partially damaged the crew of the latter being captured. About midnight a Zeppelin was seen in a Northerly direction from Camp, in the ray of a searchlight, under fire from anti-aircraft guns. The following morning the observation bar from a Zeppelin was reported as having been found in East Anglia.	
Henlow	1.10.16	—	Zeppelin clearly visible, passed over the Camp about 9.10 pm going inland in a Westerly direction. A Zeppelin was brought down later the same night at Pottersbar, North of London.	
Henlow	11.10.16	—	Battalion with Brigade Group, inspected, and marched past General Sir Bruce	

12.

Army Form C. 2118.

WAR DIARY
INTELLIGENCE SUMMARY.
(Erase heading not required.)

Instructions regarding War Diaries and Intelligence Summaries are contained in F. S. Regs., Part II. and the Staff Manual respectively. Title pages will be prepared in manuscript.

Place	Date	Hour	Summary of Events and Information	Remarks and references to Appendices
Shenlaw	2.1.17	—	Hamilton C.C.M. K.C. V.O. Commanding Northern Army on Rockwood Common B	
Rockwood	3.1.17	—	Battalion marched by road to Molesworth Station (G.C.R.) and proceeded to Bedford, going into Billets there.	44
Bedford	6.1.17	—	From London Gazette of 2.1.17 2nd Lieut. (Temporary Captain) G.B. Stansfeld to be temporarily Major (December 1st 1916)	44

/13.

I

TO: O.C. 2/5th. Battn.,

West Riding Regiment,

Newcastle.

· · · · ·

Will you please send in Secretly your
War Diary completed to date for the inspection of
the Brigade Commander.

                          W.D. Laight
                               Captain.
Newcastle.   Brigade Major.
10.12.15.   186th. Infantry Brigade.

Secret

II

To. G.O.C. 186th Infantry Brigade

War Diary completed to date
herewith, for the inspection of the G.O.C.
the Brigade.
    Please acknowledge receipt.

                    Tom Bentley Capt Adjt
                for O.C 2/5th West Riding
                             Regt.

Newcastle
11/12/15.

Secret.

TO: O.C. 2/5 th. Battn.,
     Duke of Wellington's Rgt.

....

    War Diary of the Unit under your Command returned herewith.

    It is regretted that same has been retained by this Office for so long.

                          W.O. Wright
                                Captain.
Larkhill.   Brigade Major.
19.3.16.   186th. Infantry Brigade.

Office Copy.

[Stamp: 2/5th Bn. Duke of Wellington's West Riding Regiment No. Br/6/12/c/16 Date 20/3/16]

From O.C. 2/5 D. of W. Regt.
Iz Wazguln 180th Inf Bgde
Larkhill.

20/3/16

Received your secret letter C/168/6 5/16 of 19/3/16

WM
Colonel
Comdg 2/5 Duke of Wellington's Regt

186/62

ORIGINAL

Vol I

CONFIDENTIAL

War Diary

of

2/5th Battalion Duke of Wellington's Regt.

From Jany. 10th 1914 To Jany 31st 1914.

(Volume. I.)

Army Form C. 2118.

WAR DIARY
or
INTELLIGENCE SUMMARY.
(Erase heading not required.)

Instructions regarding War Diaries and Intelligence Summaries are contained in F.S. Regs., Part II. and the Staff Manual respectively. Title pages will be prepared in manuscript.

Place	Date	Hour	Summary of Events and Information	Remarks and references to Appendices
BEDFORD.	10/1/14	9.5 a.m.	The 1/5 Duke of Wellingtons Regt entrained for Southampton Docks en route for service with the B.E.F. France. Strength. 39 Officers 992 Other Ranks (detailed list of officers + W.Os attached. marked 1.)	
SOUTHAMPTON.	"	2.45 p.m.	Arrived. Battalion sent to Rest Camp for the night.	
"	11/1/14	4.30 p.m.	Embarked for Le Havre 200 men Regtl. Transport & Stores on "S.S. Manchester Importer". Remainder of the Battalion on the S.S. "Queen Alexandra". Crossing quiet.	
LE HAVRE	12/1/14	12.30 p.m.	Disembarked. Route march to No 2 Rest Camp. Transport left at No 9. Halle, Le Havre. Under canvas at No 2 Rest Camp - weather conditions wet + cold.	
"	13/1/14	3.50 p.m.	Battalion entrained at GARE MERCHANDISE. 1st Train 1 Coy, 2nd Train 2 Coys & Transport (Headqrs.), 3rd Train 1 Coy.	
Auxi-le-Chateau	14/1/14	2 p.m.	Detrained. Route march to billets at NOEUX. Billets barns in poor condition. Severe frost	
NOEUX	22/1/14	11 a.m.	After 1 weeks efforts in completing equipment the Batt.n with the rest of the 62nd Division moved to place of concentration nearer the line. Battalion route marched to AMPLIER. arriving 6.30 p.m. 22/1/14. Distance 14 miles. Road fair.	
AMPLIER	22/1/14	6.30 p.m.	Batt.n billeted in Huts 1 mile N of village, along with 1/4 D of W.Regt. Severe frost.	
"	23/1/14	11 a.m.	Route march continued to BUS-les-ARTOIS. arrived 2.35 p.m. Billets, barns in fair condition, previously occupied by 3rd Div.n. Severe frost. Road fair considering days around of transport.	
BUS-les-ARTOIS	23/1/14 to 31/1/14		Battalion from 24th to 31st found working parties of 530 other ranks for new Artillery dumps etc at ACHEUX, + BEAUSSART. From the 25th to 31st parties of Officers & NCO's went daily for instruction in the trenches to 96th + 114th 2nd Brig.s occupying the front from BEAUMONT HAMEL to South of HEBUTERNE. The severe frost continued throughout this period	

J.D. Best Lt Col Comdg 1/5 D of W Regt.

1577   Wt.W.10791/1773   500,000   1/15   D.D.&L.   A.D.S.S./Forms/C. 2118.

Boo Auteuil 4/2/14

Vol 2

WAR DIARY
of
7/5 Bn Duke of Wellingtons Regt.
from 1st Feby 1917 to 28th Feby 1917.

Volume II.

Vol 2

WAR DIARY

of

1/5 B[n] Duke of Wellington's Regt.

from 1st Feby 1914 to 28th Feby 1914.

Volume II.

Original

2/5th Duke of
Wellington. Regt.

Army Form C. 2118.

Instructions regarding War Diaries and Intelligence
Summaries are contained in F. S. Regs., Part II.
and the Staff Manual respectively. Title pages
will be prepared in manuscript.

WAR DIARY
INTELLIGENCE SUMMARY.
(Erase heading not required.)

Place	Date	Hour	Summary of Events and Information	Remarks and references to Appendices
BUS-les-ARTOIS	1/2/17 to 2/2/17		Working Parties found for V Corps on new Amm: dumps & roads up to 5/2/17.	
	3/2/17	11 p.m	63rd Divn (R.N.Div.) attacked on front N.E. of BEAUMONT HAMEL + W. of BEAUCOURT & took Artillery Alley, PUISIEUX + River Trenches & 200 prisoners of 301st (J.R. 18th Div.) & 3 machine guns.	
	4/2/17		Two German counter attacks on the 63rd Divn. repulsed.	
	5/2/17	10.45 p.m	A & B Coys in the trenches opposite HEBUTERNE. 26th + 1st + 5th Brigades for instruction. 711 N.E. BENTLEY reported as missing, leaving sine and with a patrol of No 4 Post Lane. They came upon a party of the enemy in a trench & after taking one prisoner were returning to our lines when the prisoner was shot dead by the enemy. The Corporal of the Party was also wiped out & Lieut: an NCO held up into German wire. This occurred during the night of the 5th/6th Feb at about K.11.a.24.	
	6/2/17 to 7/2/17		C & D Coys in the trenches opposite HEBUTERNE and 56th + 58th Brigades for instruction.	
BUS "	7/2/17 to 11/2/17		Batt" again finding working parties of about 300 men daily for V Corps Amm: dumps etc.	
"	12/2/17		Batt" left BUS at 2.45 p.m by rail & road for BEAUMONT HAMEL & took over portion of trenches Sector R.3 from the 1st/18th Dorsets. No casualties during relief. A & B Coys in the line with hqrs in TEN TREE ALLEY South of SERRE with C + D Coys in support along with Batt" Adjms at BURN WORK in BEAUMONT HAMEL. TL/4 Duffy W" was on our left & the 155th Brig on our right. The Batt" had 6 other ranks killed + 5 other ranks wounded during the tour which was 4 days. The severe frost which had continued without break from Jan 1st gave place to a night & rain on the 15/2/17 & the whole trench system became most difficult for transit. Posts & tracks being up to 2 feet deep in mud.	

WAR DIARY
INTELLIGENCE SUMMARY

Army Form C. 2118.

Place	Date	Hour	Summary of Events and Information	Remarks and references to Appendices
BEAUMONT HAMEL	13/2/17	5 a.m.	63rd Div. on our right attacked from BAILLESCOURT FARM & took SWAN TRENCH with 400 prisoners.	
"	"	4 p.m.	7/6 D.L.I. Regt relieve the Batt. Owing to the snow the whole of the ground took on quite a different aspect & guides though working hard could not get to post BRINDLE BITCH what it was impossible to relieve until the following night. The relief was not completed until 9 a.m. 18/2/17 when Batt. arrived in billets at MAILLY-MAILLET.	
MAILLY-MAILLET	18/2/17		Batt. in billets. Intelligence reports that the enemy counter attacked the 63rd Div. (who had taken SWAN TRENCH) from the WUNDTWERK but otherwise being caught by our artillery barrage.	
"	19/2/17 to 22/2/17		Batt. on I Corps working parties. R.E. & Amm. Dumps. 350 men being found daily.	
MAILLY WOODS EAST.	22/2/17		Batt. moved from MAILLY into OLDHAM CAMP at MAILLY WOODS EAST. Major R.E. NEGUS 2nd in command to the Batt. took over command of the 1/8 West Yorkshire Regt, vice Lt. Col. Hepworth.	
"	23/2/17 to 24/2/17		Batt. on I Corps working parties at R.E. & Amm. Dumps, 350 men daily.	
"	25/2/17	2 a.m.	As enemy were reported to have vacated SERRE the Brigade was warned to be ready to move from 5 a.m. onwards to push out patrols towards (A) BEAUREGARD DOVECOTE & (C) PUISIEUX. At 5 a.m. the 184th Bde were to push on to PUISIEUX supported by mainbody of 184th Bde. The 63rd (R.N.) Div. on the right & 4th Div. on the left were to act similarly. 9/6 found to be unoccupied they were to push on to 184th Bde. GREEN DUMP. Q.11.c.5.3 at 8 a.m. for carrying parties &c.	
"	"	2:10 a.m.	Batt. ordered to report to 184th Bde. GREEN DUMP. Q.11.c.5.3 at 8 a.m. for carrying parties &c.	
"	"	6:45 a.m.	Batt. moved off, reported to Staff Capt. 184th Inf. Bde. at GREEN DUMP & was used for carrying parties	

Army Form C. 2118.

WAR DIARY
INTELLIGENCE SUMMARY.
(Erase heading not required.)

Instructions regarding War Diaries and Intelligence Summaries are contained in F. S. Regs., Part II. and the Staff Manual respectively. Title pages will be prepared in manuscript.

Place	Date	Hour	Summary of Events and Information	Remarks and references to Appendices
BEAUMONT HAMEL	26/2/19		& making of forward dumps at TANK ALLEY & DOUBTFUL POST. also for bringing up cable. At night parties were also found for carrying forward rations for 189th Brig. The Batt. was quartered for the night in Y. RAVINE (2 Coys) + dugouts near RED DUMP.	
	"	10 a.m.	Batt. again employed carrying & digging trenches for 189th Brig at GREEN DUMP.	
	"		Batt. notified that 186th Inf Brig will relieve 189th Inf Brig.	
	"	1.45 p.m.	Orders received from 189th Brig (to whom Batt. was temp. attached) to relieve 1/4 K.O.Y.L.I. who were occupying the GUDGEON TRENCH S.E. of PUSIEUX with 3 Coys & the WUNDTWERK 1Coy + H.Q.etc.	
	"	4 p.m.	Batt. left dugouts at RED DUMP & marched via BEAUCOURT & PUSIEUX Rd to above position. The relief was completed by 6.5 a.m. Casualties during relief being 3 men wounded.	
WUNDT WERK	27/2/19	3 p.m.	Our patrols report PUSIEUX, + ORCHARD ALLEY held by enemy will about 4 machine guns.	
	"		Orders received from 186th Inf Brig to hold ORCHARD ALLEY + push out posts to Point L.15.c.4.4 + L.15.d.3.5. in SUNKEN ROAD running from PUSIEUX to ACHIET-LE-PETIT.	
	"	8 p.m.	Captured ORCHARD TRENCH C.O reported to Brig.: "Have captured ORCHARD ALLEY. Patrols pushing out towards SUNKEN Rd".	
	"		This was carried out by 2 Patrols of "D" Coy. + 1 Patrol of "A" Coy. and 15 Bn.y + supported by D. Coy.	
	28/2/19	12.30 a.m.	Patrols pushed on + established posts in SUNKEN ROAD Points L.15.a.4.4 + L.15.d.3.5. Casualties. 3 killed + 8 wounded.	
	"	9.25 a.m.	G.O.C. Brig. wired his appreciation of above. During the day the positions were consolidated + touch obtained with 2nd Bn R Warwicks 4 Div on left & 1/6 D of W Rgt on Right.	
ENGLEBELMER	2/3/19			

J. O. Beatty. Lt Colonel
Comdg 1/5 Duke of Wellington Rgt.

2/5th Bn. Duke of Wellington's Regiment.
ROLL OF OFFICERS & W.O.s BY SENIORITY

Lieut-Colonel. T.A.D. Best, D.S.O.   Commanding Officer.

Major. R.E. Negus.   Battalion 2nd in Command.
Major. G.B. Faulder.   O.C. "A" Company.

Captain. T. Bentley.   Adjutant.
ø. Captain. W. Graham.
Captain. G. Glover.   O.C. "C" Company.
Captain. J. Walker.   O.C. "B"   "
Captain. T. Goodall.   O.C. "D"   "
Captain. A.R. Haigh.   2nd in Command. "A" Coy.
Captain. W. Shaw.   "   "   "   "D" "
Captain. G.L. Tinker.   "   "   "   "B" "
Captain. C.A.W. Williams.   "   "   "   "C" "

Lieut. T.P. Crosland.   Transport Officer.
x. Lieut. A.M. Balfour.   Battalion Bombing Officer.
x. Lieut. P.R. Ridley.
Lieut. H.S. Jackson.   Lewis Gun Officer.
Lieut. W.L. Thomas.
Lieut. H.G. Hodgkinson.
Lieut. L.D. Goldseller.   Battalion Signalling Officer.
Lieut. J.A. Haigh.   "   Sniping Officer.
Lieut. O. Walker.
W. Lieut. K.C.M. Teather.
W. Lieut. K.B. Caldicott.

2/Lieut. T.C. Jacobs.
2/Lieut. G.V. Bernays.
2/Lieut. H.A. Simmonds.   Trench Tramway Officer.
&. 2/Lieut. J.F. Waters.
2/Lieut. W.A. Croxson.
2/Lieut. F.W. Butterworth.
2/Lieut. H.H. Oldham.
2/Lieut. A.M. Fisher.
2/Lieut. N.E. Bentley.

<u>Medical Officer.</u>   Captain. W. Robertson.
<u>C. of E. Chaplain.</u> Captain the Rev. Thornhill.
<u>Quarter Master.</u>   Qr.Mr. & Hon. Lieut. P.E. Hammond.

ø. Attached from 6th Bn. Durham Light Infantry.
x.   "   "   1st Northern Cyclist Battalion.
W.   "   "   2/7th Cyclist Battalion, Welsh Regiment.
&.   "   "   2/1st Northern Cyclist Battalion.

9323 A/Rgl.Sgt.Mjr. B. Earle.   Regimental Sergeant Major.
3005 Coy.Sgt.Mjr. J. Woodcock.   Coy. Sgt. Major. "B" Coy.
2703   "   "   " G. Gannon.   "   "   "   "A" Coy.
3456   "   "   " R. Dawson.   "   "   "   "D" Coy.
3749   "   "   " T. Payne.   "   "   "   "C" Coy.
2620 Rgl.Qr.Mr.Sgt. Kaye. C.R.   Regl. Qr. Mr. Sergeant.

Feb. 4th 1917.

T. Bentley Capt/Adjt
Lieut-Colonel
Commdg. 2/5th Bn. Duke of Wellington's Regt.

Vol 3

Confidential

WAR DIARY.
of
2/5 Bⁿ Duke of Wellington's Regt.
VOLUME III
March 1917.

Original

2/5 M Bn Duke of Wellington's Regt

WAR DIARY

Army Form C. 2118.

INTELLIGENCE SUMMARY.

(Erase heading not required.)

Instructions regarding War Diaries and Intelligence Summaries are contained in F.S. Regs., Part II. and the Staff Manual respectively. Title pages will be prepared in manuscript.

Place	Date	Hour	Summary of Events and Information	Remarks and references to Appendices
WUNDTWERK	1/3/17	2 a.m.	The 22nd Manchester Regt commenced to relieve the Batt. Owing to the difficult nature of the ground + the extreme darkness the relief was not completed until 4.45am. Rapt. the guides worked very well + were complimented by the relieving Batt. The casualty only occurred during the relief. Total casualties for the tour were 5 killed + 12 wounded.	
ENGELBELMER	2/3/17	1 pm	Battalion took over billets formerly occupied by the 63rd (R.N.) Division.	
"	3/3/17		Battalion cleaning up etc.	
"	4/3/17		500 men of Batt. sent to FORCEVILLE to dig trench system of trenches similar to German position at ACHIET LE PETIT, which 62nd Div. is to attack.	
"	5/3/17 & 7/3/17		Batt Practice attack for ACHIET LE PETIT. Snow on the 5/3/17, other days had been very wet + muddy.	
"	8/3/17	12.30 pm	Batt. left to encamp at PELICAN CAMP BEAUMONT HAMEL.	
PELICAN CAMP	9/3/17		Batt. warned as tactical reserve for 189th Bgd. who are in the line at MIRAUMONT	
"	9/3/17 to 14/3/17		500 men at work daily under R.E. on the BEAUCOURT Roads + under Can. Rly. Troops on railway at BEAUMONT HAMEL and BEAUCOURT. Remainder of Batt. on salvage work in BEAUMONT HAMEL neighb.	
"	15/3/17	3-15 p.m.	Batt. left PELICAN CAMP for MIRAUMONT + took over line 3 miles S.E. of ACHIET LE PETIT from 7/5 KOYLI. 2 Coy, 7/4 Y & L. 1 Coy. + 8th NF; 1 Coy. Transport was heavily shelled proceeding through ACHIET MIRAUMONT. 3 Drivers being wounded + 1 mule killed + 2 others wounded.	

Army Form C. 2118.

WAR DIARY
INTELLIGENCE SUMMARY.
(Erase heading not required.)

Instructions regarding War Diaries and Intelligence Summaries are contained in F. S. Regs., Part II. and the Staff Manual respectively. Title pages will be prepared in manuscript.

Place	Date	Hour	Summary of Events and Information	Remarks and references to Appendices
MIRAUMONT	16/3/17		Position was heavily shelled during the day particularly RESURRECTION TRENCH occupied by B.Coy who had 5 killed & 4 wounded in their forward bombing post during the day. The 7/4 D of W. Regt. were on our right & the 7/4 D of W. on the left during this tour.	
"	17/3/17	4 a.m.	The 7/4 D of W. on right reported that the occupied an enemy trench 300 yds in front of their line without opposition & B Coy reported tht at the same time patrols found the ground opposite them for about 300 yds free from enemy. C.O. ordered B Coy to push on through ACHIET LE PETIT & occupy sunken road North of village. This B Coy did occupying Sunken Road & consolidating it at 6.50 am. Immediately the coy were through the village (where the resistance was not great) the enemy barrage descended on the northern portion of it, but the Coy were already through & only two men were slightly wounded. The remaining coys also moved forward & occupied RESURRECTION & QUICK trenches in support. About 1.30 p.m. parties of enemy were seen to retire round eastern edge of LOG EAST WOOD & several chargers were blown up in the BIHUCOURT line running South of LOG EAST WOOD.	
ACHIET LE PETIT	"	5.15 p.m.	Instructions received from 186" Inf Brig to move forward & occupy line of BIHUCOURT TRENCH & BACHIET LE GRAND, to cut gaps in wire to allow through the cavalry, also one coy to push forward & occupy GOMIECOURT.	
		4 p.m.	Batt moved towards this end. BIHUCOURT LINE to be taken from left by night by A C & B Coys. D Coy to push forward to GOMIECOURT. C Coy & B Coy to each send a road through the wire.	
		11-50 p.m.	C.O reported to Brig: above line occupied & wire cut at 11 p.m. There was only slight opposition, but the wire was a formidable obstacle, there being five belts each 10 feet thick & about 30 yds apart.	

1577 Wt.W10791/1773 500,000 1/15 D. D. & L. A.D.S.S./Forms/C. 2118.

Army Form C. 2118.

WAR DIARY
INTELLIGENCE SUMMARY
(Erase heading not required.)

Instructions regarding War Diaries and Intelligence Summaries are contained in F.S. Regs., Part II. and the Staff Manual respectively. Title pages will be prepared in manuscript.

Place	Date	Hour	Summary of Events and Information	Remarks and references to Appendices
ACHIET le PETIT.	18/3/17.	4.30 a.m.	D. Coy. occupied GOMIECOURT experiencing slight machine gun fire. At 9.30 a.m. the cavalry arrived passing through the BIHUCOURT line forward towards ST. LEGER etc. Owing to the shortening of the line the Batt: did not move past GOMIECOURT, the 4th Div. on left, & the 19th Div. on right having joined up with each other at ERVILLERS. Since the evening of 16/17 when the enemy shelled ACHIET le PETIT his artillery was very quiet until the 21st.	
"	19/3/17 to 22/3/17.		Batt: stood fast on ground occupied, resting & improving accommodation, there being plenty of material (left behind by the enemy) for this purpose. Though all existing accommodation without exception & the majority of roads had been destroyed. Several dug-out entrances were found to contain mines, & important road junctions had been blown up.	
"	23/3/17 to 31/3/17.		Batt: employed on road & railway repairs at ACHIET le PETIT, ACHIET le GRAND, PUISIEUX, GOMIECOURT & on R.Y.A. dumps at BEHAGNIES. The Batt being distributed as follows during this period :- Hdqrs & wagon lines ACHIET-le-PETIT, A Coy. LOGEAST WOOD, B & C. Coys. ACHIET le GRAND, & D. Coy at GOMIECOURT. During rifle grenade practice Capt. Goodall, 2/Ld Oldham & three NCO's were accidentally wounded by the premature explosion of a Mills Rifle Grenade evidently through defective mechanism in the Grenade. Lieut P.R. Ridley was awarded the Military Cross & 2/Lt H. Priestly the Military Medal for their participation in the attack on ORCHARD ALLEY, PUISIEUX Feby 24/25 1917.	See extracts from D.O's attached & marked A.
BEHAGNIES.	2/4/17.			T.D. Best Lt. Colonel Comdg. 1/5 Duke of Wellington's

ORIGINAL

Confidential

WAR DIARY.

2/5 Bn. Duke of Wellingtons Regt.

Volume IV.

April 1st — April 30th. 1917.

Army Form C. 2118.

WAR DIARY
or
INTELLIGENCE SUMMARY.
(Erase heading not required.)

Instructions regarding War Diaries and Intelligence Summaries are contained in F. S. Regs., Part II. and the Staff Manual respectively. Title pages will be prepared in manuscript.

Place	Date	Hour	Summary of Events and Information	Remarks and references to Appendices
BEHAGNIES	1/4/17		Batt. moved from ACHIET le PETIT, ACHIET le GRAND & GOMIECOURT into BEHAGNIES.	
"	2/4/17		Two men of C. Coy accidentally wounded by explosion of bomb or hidden German device in billet.	
"	3/4/17	4 p.m.	German aeroplane destroyed two of our observation balloons at BEHAGNIES & bomb fired on escort.	
"	4/4/17 to 8/4/17		Batt. on working parties at R.A. Comm'n dumps & roads.	
"	9/4/17		Bgde. practice attack for coming attack on BULLECOURT.	
"	10/4/17	5 a.m.	Batt. left for concentration of troops behind ECOUST ready to move through as advanced guard in the event of the Anzac Corps who were attacking breaking through. Troops were ordered back at 7.15 a.m. as attack had been postponed	
"	11/4/17	5 a.m.	Batt. again left for concentration behind ECOUST. Anzacs take both 1st & 2nd objectives but later in the day, another and 1 Batt. with other units of Bgde. billeted at MORY.	
MORY	12/4/17		Third Lieut. & 12 other ranks slept with similar parties from other units of the Bgde. successfully fired Bangalore torpedoes in the enemy wire W. of BULLECOURT. The Div. Comm'r expressed his appreciation of this work.	
"	14/4/17		Lieut L.D. Goldsteller the Batt. Sig. Officer was mortally wounded whilst reconnoitring the German position S.W. of BULLECOURT. He was accompanied by four Batt. Guides who were able to carry him back to ECOUST. As a result of this 10536 Pte. E.E. Reed was awarded the Military Medal & No 5222 Pte. C. Crabtree & No 5160 Private C. Chapman were mentioned in Divisional Orders.	See Appendix B attached.
"	15/4/17		Lieut L.D. Goldsteller was buried by the Jewish Chaplain opposite MORY ABBEY (B22 a 6 8 - Sheet 57 c N.W)	

WAR DIARY
or
INTELLIGENCE SUMMARY.

(Erase heading not required.)

Army Form C. 2118.

Place	Date	Hour	Summary of Events and Information	Remarks and references to Appendices
MORY	14/4/17		During the afternoon the enemy shelled the Eastern outskirts of MORY where the Batt was bivouaced & caused casualties of 3 men killed & 9 men wounded in the Batt. Camps were then moved into the area S.W. of MORY.	
MORY.	15/4/17 to 30/4/17		Batt. was employed along with other units of the Bgde refairing MORY road, the carrying of gasshells forward for Special Coy R.E., digging in of cable between L'HOMME MORT and ECOUST also on felling in craters in MORY & ECOUST. During this period special training was carried out in practising the attack on the HINDENBERG line at BULLECOURT.	

MORY. 2/5/14.

Geo. Best. Lt Colonel
Comdg. 1/5 Duke of Wellington Rgt.

Appendix A.

Certified true copy of extract from Div. Orders.
Behagnies 2/4/17.
[signature] Lt Col.
Comdg 2/5 D of W R[?]

HONOURS AND REWARDS
   Under authority granted by His Majesty the King, the Field Marhsal, Commanding-in-Chief has awarded decorations to following Officer.

MILITARY CROSS
   Lieutenant. P.R. Ridley, 2/5th West Riding Regiment for the following action.-
   " On the evening of 27/28th Feb.1917 was in charge if a party of three Officers' patrols each of one Officer and 15 Other Ranks, detailed to rush ORCHARD ALLEY from GUDEON TRENCH, Lieut.Ridley was responsible for maintaining the direction, marching on a compass bearing for 500 yards across unknown and difficult country.
       This Officer led his party with great dash shooting one German and capturing another on entering the trench. He showed considerable coolness and ability in the attack, and in organising the defence of the trench.
           (Fifth Army A.M.S. to C.in-C. H.R./742/752.).
              (Vide. Div.Order No.340).

HONOURS AND REWARDS
   The Commander of the V.Corps, under authority delegated to him, hhas awarded the Military Medal to the undermentioned N.C.O. -
" No.8397 L/Cpl. Hubert.Priestley, 2/5th West Riding Regt for the following action.-
   " On the evening of the Feb.27th-28th 1917, was in Command of a Bombing Section which formed part of a party ordered to rush ORCHARD ALLEY from GUDEON TRENCH. He led his Bombers with great dash and courage and though wounded in the head by a Bomb continued to bomb his way along the trench and led his men in a most gallant manner.
       His example undoubtedly encouraged the remainder who were then taking part in their first attack.
           (V.Corps. M.M. 197, dated March 10th 1917).
              (Vide. Div.Order No.307 of 16-3-17).

Appendix B.

HONOURS AND REWARDS

The Commander of the Fifth Corps, under authority delegated to him, has awarded the Military Medal to the undermentioned.-

No. 5036 Private Edward Cyril Rust, West Riding Regt for the following action.-
" At ECOUST ST.MEIN, on the night of the 14th/15th April 1917, Private Rust was one of a patrol of four under LIEUT.L.D.GOLDSELLER reconnoitring the S.W. corner of BULLECOURT.

The party had got through the enemy's wire when they were discovered and fired on. One man was wounded in the hand and LIEUT.GOLDSELLER shot through the stomach. Pte.Rust assisted by Privates. Crabtree, Chapman and Carter carried LIEUT.GOLDSELLER into a German trench inside the wire, the nearest cover available, that portion of the trench being fortunately unoccupied.

Pte.Carter was sent to get a stretcher, and the other three remained in the trench., Very Lights going up on each side of them for about an hour.

They then carried LIEUT.GOLDSELLER through the wire and back towards our lines, meeting the stretcher party about 200 yards from the German lines.

During the whole time they were returning they were under heavy sniping and bursts of machine gun fire. LIEUT.GOLDSELLER died shortly after arrival at Dressing Station.
(V.Corps Letter M.M.320 dated 24.4.17).
(Vide. Div.Order No.464 dated 27.4.17).

OPERATIONS - MERITORIOUS SERVICE DURING

The General Officer Commanding wishes to place on record his high appreciation of the gallant conduct of the following men, which has been brought to his notice by Brigadier-Generals and Commanding Officers of the formations concerned.
   No.5222 PRIVATE. C.CRABTREE. West Riding Regiment.
   No.5100.PRIVATE. C. CHAPMAN.   "   "   "/
(Vide. Div.Order No.466 dated 27-4-17).

Original

Vol. 5 182/22

Confidential

WAR DIARY.
2/5TH BN DUKE of WELLINGTON'S REGIMENT

MAY 1ST 1917 to MAY 31ST 1917.

Volume 5.

WEST RIDING

59.
7 sheets

2/5 Duke of Wellington Regt.

Army Form C. 2118.

WAR DIARY
or
INTELLIGENCE SUMMARY.
(Erase heading not required.)

Place	Date	Hour	Summary of Events and Information	Remarks and references to Appendices
MORY	1/5/17	9.0AM	Coys employed in making dumps/posts & specialist training	H.S.f
		12.30PM 45 2-4PM	Coys went over miniature trench system of Bullecourt fully depicting the roads, trenches & barrage lines.	
MORY	2/5/17	9 to 12.30	Enlisted Ecemay & preparations for going into the line. Afternoon Coys again went over miniature trench system of Bullecourt.	
		9.15PM	Batt marched to ECOUST (Embankment) when they dropped coats for getting over trenches & bombs. They then formed up on tape line Ref map 1:10000 1st Coust St MIEN U26d99 to U2tG71 all was completed by 1.30AM & without casualties. Tanks followed the Batt down from L'Homme Mort to Ecoust.	H.S.f
ECOUST	3/5/17	3.45AM	Zero hour. At zero hour minus 8 minutes Batt moved forward to attack HINDENBERG LINE WEST of BULLECOURT. A heavy barrage commenced at Zero. A Coy reached their objective & held it until 4.0PM when they were counter attacked & bombed out, they retired on to Embankment.	
			B, C & D Coys came under heavy shell, rifle & Machine Gun fire & were held up in front of Enemy front line trench, small parties holding out in shell holes until after dusk when they retired to Embankment. Batt suffered heavy casualties. The following officers were killed, Capt & Adj	H.S.f

WAR DIARY or INTELLIGENCE SUMMARY

2/5 Duke of Wellingtons Army Form C. 2118.

Place	Date	Hour	Summary of Events and Information	Remarks and references to Appendices
~~Mory~~ Ecoust	3/5/17 continued		BENTLEY, LIEUT O Walker. Missing believed killed. ~~Lieut~~ Heut-posts ~~that~~ Missing Capt G Glover, Lieut G Reilly M.C. Heut E.T Sykes, Heut Heaton, Heut Doronnt & Hutton. Wounded Capt W Staw. Heuts Kirk, A & Simmons. Shell shock Lieut K.C Leathery Capt Walker.	H.S.1. Killed 2 N.C.O.'r Men Killed 123 Missing 2 Wounded 275.
		8.0 PM	See posts were put out in W26 C&D under Capt Goodall. Lieut Haigh went out with stretcher bearers to bring in wounded.	
Ecoust	4/5/17		Batt still holding the line, wounded dribbled in all day. Shelling was heavy. At night Batt were relieved by 2/6th & 2/7th Duke of Wellingtons & marched East by companies to Mory.	H.S.1.
			Cops in to Camps. During relief there were no casualties. Arrived MORY cops about 2.30 AM next day	H.S.1
Mory Cops	5/5/17 morning		Batt rested & moved camps across MORY, STLEDGER Rd. Afternoon, Took steps to reorganise.	H.S.1
		7.0 PM	Draft of 5 officers arrived, consisting of Lieuts Binley, Moscow & 2/Lieuts G Booth, Black & B.S Jodd.	H.S.1
Mory Cops	6/5/17		Church parade & Training.	H.S.1
Mory Cops	7/5/17		Batt employed in reorganising & Training. Corps Commander & General Braithwaite inspected Camp & Battalion	H.S.1
		6.30 PM	Marched to ERVILLERS into Camp.	
ERVILLERS	8/5/17		Battalion bathed, carried out Specialist training & Interior Economy.	H.S.1
ERVILLERS	9/5/17	9.0 AM	Specialist Training. Some officers attended lecture by Army Commander.	H.S.1

WAR DIARY or INTELLIGENCE SUMMARY

Army Form C. 2118.

2/5 Duke of Wellington's Regt

Place	Date	Hour	Summary of Events and Information	Remarks and references to Appendices
ERVILLERS	9/5/17	3.0pm	C/o Relieved N.C.O.s & Men on reverts made by Army Commander.	H.S.J
continued		8.0pm	Party of 8 men & 2 officers (Capt Robertson R.A.M. & Lieut Calvert) went to ECOUST in search for wounded.	H.S.J
ERVILLERS	10/5/17	1.0AM	Search Party returned, they had no casualties & brought in 4 wounded 2 of our own Regt.	H.S.J
		9.0AM	Specialist training through day.	
ERVILLERS	11/5/17 & 12/5/17		Battalion Carried out Specialist training, also provided 3 working parties of Officers 50 men each for unloading Ammunition at Divisional dump E.RVILLERS.	H.S.J
ERVILLERS	12/5/17	9.0AM	Interior economy & preparing for line	
		7.45PM	Battalion C/o ERVILLERS for ECOUST. Maj Fawlds was in Charge. Strength 2 companies. Coys Arrived ECOUST without being shelled at 10.30pm. Relieved 2/6th local Yorkshire Regt. took over 3 posts in no area & remands of Battalion on Embankment, First Leave for Battalion Commenced.	H.S.J
ECOUST	14/5/17		Holding the line by posts as on 13/5/17. Companies on Embankment improved shelter for ship.	
		11.0pm	Relieved posts in road area from A Coy, who also relieved 1/7th Do W's from darken Rd with 30 Men put out our own post officers in Charge Lieut Mascow & Lieut R Bowel. There were no casualties throughout the day.	H.S.J

Army Form C. 2118.

WAR DIARY
or
INTELLIGENCE SUMMARY.

1/5 Duke of Wellington's Regt

(Erase heading not required.)

Place	Date	Hour	Summary of Events and Information	Remarks and references to Appendices
ECOUST	15/5/17	3.0 AM	Still holding the line in Sunken Road & posts. Men were engaged in putting out wire & trench posts in front of embankment, during the day a battalion dump was formed, a Composite Battalion formed from 1/5 & 1/4 D of W under 1/Col Chamberlain. Lieut Moore & 2 other Rks went on patrol towards BULLECOURT. Enemy in Bullecourt they found on by snipers & M.G's & had to return after reaching the enemy second Belt of wire. Sunken Rd was heavily shelled during day & heavy sniping & Enfilading Rd M.G. fire enemy heavy gas bombardment took place between 1.0 AM & 5 P.M. Lieut Crosland was gassed when bringing up rations.	H.S.9
ECOUST	16/5/17		1/5th D of W relieved rear posts. D Coy relieved A Coy from Sunken Road. 2/Lt Black D & 2/Lt Jack R.A.M.C. in charge. News was received that Bullecourt was to be evacuated by the Germans. At 9.0 AM Lieut Black and out 2 fighting patrols to ascertain whether news was correct, they were held up short of Crucifix by snipers M.G. fire & had to return about 10.0 P.M. Sergt Schofield Hulse & L/Cpl Johnson died covered work. Three men were wounded by a sniper in Sunken Road: A reinforced was established during night in new trench running from Sunken Road towards Crucifix. One man was wounded in this post. Sniper infilading Sunken Rd was engaged & silenced for a while by L.G. fire.	H.S.d

Army Form C. 2118.

WAR DIARY
or
INTELLIGENCE SUMMARY.
(Erase heading not required.)

7/5 Duke of Wellingtons Regt

Place	Date	Hour	Summary of Events and Information	Remarks and references to Appendices
ECOUST	17/5/17		A Coy. relieved D Coy in another Rd. Lieut Sutcliffe & 2/Lt Watkinson in charge. RE's continued wiring in front of Sunken Rd & B continued trench towards crucifix. 58th Div on our right attacked & captured the whole of Bullecourt. Patrols were sent out by us from Sunken Rd to gain touch with 58th Div, they succeeded in the locality. Sergt Ellis A coy was in charge & did good work. Sniping still active up Sunken Rd, one casualty, being caused.	H.S.J
ECOUST	18/5/17		D Coy relieved A Coy from Sunken Rd, Capt Williams & 2/Lieut Booker in charge. May Sawden took a bombing patrol under Cpl Whitehead out to Crucifix, they then went up Hindenburg trench W of BULLECOURT & about 100 yds round trend to pt U2.C1.15. where they encountered enemy, a short fight with bombs & rifle grenades took place & the patrol returned. No casualties.	H.S.J
ECOUST	19/5/17		2/Lt: B Coy relieved D coy from Sunken Rd. A Coy took over rear posts, wiring was continued in front of embankment. By D & C established a block in fort Hindenburg trench at St U2, C2.4.	H.S.J
ECOUST	20/5/17		Shelling quiet during day. 10.30 p.m. Battalion relieved by 1/5 Yorks Lancs. Relief completed at 1.0 p.m. 21/5/17. Battalion marched to COURCELLES via ERVILLERS. arrived at 3.30 a.m. No casualties during relief	H.S.J
COURCELLES	21/5/17		Battalion bathed & otherwise recovering.	H.S.J

Army Form C. 2118.

WAR DIARY
or
INTELLIGENCE SUMMARY.
(Erase heading not required.)

2/5 Duke of Wellingtons Regt.

Place	Date	Hour	Summary of Events and Information	Remarks and references to Appendices
COURCELLES	27/5/17 to 28/5/17		Draft of 62 men arrived from Base. Battalion Employed in Specialist training, musketry on Range & Physical training.	H.S.J
COURCELLES	29/5/17	10 AM	Battalion marched to ACHIET-LE-PETIT into camp for Divisional rest.	H.S.J
		2:0 PM	Employed in making football field & training ring.	
ACHIET LE PETIT	30/5/17 to 31/5/17		Specialist training, Bayonet fighting, 50 men on fatigue at Range, afternoons off for Sports. No 5108 Pte. Chapman C was awarded "Croix de Guerre" for good work done at ECOUST when out with Lieut L.B. Goldallon on 14/4/19.	H.S.J

1st June 1917.

T/Lt Col
2/5 Duke of Wellington's Regt.

CONFIDENTIAL

Vol 6

2/5TH BATTALION DUKE OF WELLINGTON'S REGIMENT

WAR DIARY

JUNE 1ST TO JUNE 30TH 1917

Volume 6

Original

WAR DIARY
or
INTELLIGENCE SUMMARY.

Army Form C. 2118.

1/5 Duke of Wellingtons R/g

Place	Date	Hour	Summary of Events and Information	Remarks and references to Appendices
ACHIET LE PETIT	1/6/17		Division in Rest. Specialist Training. Capt Sykes & 9 other ORs arrived from leave	#S.1
	2/6/17		Specialist Training	#S.8
ACHIET LE PETIT	3/6/17		Divisional Church of England service at ACHIET LE GRAND by Bishop Gwynne, Deputy Chaplain General	#S.9
ACHIET LE PETIT	4/6/17 to 10/6/17		Batt on Specialist Training. 3,225 men on working parts at ACHIET LE GRAND on all weekdays. June 6th No 241742 L/Cpl Johnson G was awarded M.M. for good work above whilst Battalion held the line from May 13 to 20. June 11th 7/2nd Wasdlove & 32 other Ranks joined Batt.	#S.9
ACHIET LE PETIT	12/6/17		Battalion took part in Brigade practice attack on ACHIET LE PETIT & finished at 12.0 AM.	#S.7
ACHIET LE PETIT	13/6/17		Training in forming up on tape lines. 7/Lt Harris & 6 other ORs joined Battalion from base	#S.9
		8.59 PM	Brigade practice alarm for moving up to assault line of defence into Support. Battalion arrived at Brigade Starting point no 39 7 minutes from Zero. Men inoculated	
ACHIET LE PETIT	June 14, 15 & 15th		Training. 14th Final for Course completion. 15th Battalion bathed.	#S.9
	June 16th		Training. Batt held a Gymkhana for Officers of Brigade, the Batt winning 4 events out of 5	#S.9
ACHIET LE PETIT	17/6/17	10.45AM	Church parade in Crater.	
ACHIET-LE-PETIT	19/6/17		Brigade Sports. Batt obtained most points in the Brigade.	9B7
ACHIET-LE-PETIT	21/6/17		2/Lieuts G Dyson, W O Davis & 80 OR reported from base	9B7 9B7
ACHIET.LE PETIT	22/6/17 to 29/6/17		Training	9A9

WAR DIARY
or
INTELLIGENCE SUMMARY.
(Erase heading not required.)

Army Form C. 2118.

1/5 Duke of Wellington's Regt

Place	Date	Hour	Summary of Events and Information	Remarks and references to Appendices
ACHIET-LE-PETIT	26/8/17		Batt. moves from camp at 2.20 p.m. to RESERVE CAMP at VAULX relieving 10th K.R.R. (20th Div)	G.87.
VAULX	27/8/17		Batt. left camp at 9.40 p.m. for the front line in V.29 c & d (HQ C.5. a.2.3.) relieving 12th Kings Liverpool Regt. Relief completed without casualties at 1.50 a.m. 28/8/17.	G.87. G.87.
In the line	28/8/17	3.8/8/17 10 p.m.	Batt. holding the line. Casualties two — 1 killed & 1 wounded.	G.87.

H.O. Best Lt Col.
1/5 Duke of Wellington's Regt

2/5 Duke of Wellington's Regt.

SECRET

Vol 7

War Diary.

2/5th Bn. Duke of Wellington's Regiment.

July 1917.

Volume 7.

WAR DIARY
or
INTELLIGENCE SUMMARY.

(Erase heading not required.)

Army Form C. 2118.

2/5 Duke of Wellingtons
July 1917.

Place	Date	Hour	Summary of Events and Information	Remarks and references to Appendices
NOREUIL	1.7.17		Batt holding the line in LEFT NOREUIL SECTOR. Relieved by 1/4 Dow & go into Support.	#S.J
NOREUIL	2.7.17 to 4.7.17		Batt in Support in SUNKEN RD LEFT NOREUIL SECTOR. Employed in carrying parties, cleaning	
	5.7.17		lines at WINDY CORNER & digging new trench in front line. Relieved by 4/KOYLI. H.S.J	
			& marched back to Camp at H5d. NE BEUGNATRE. 5.7.17.	
BEUGNATRE	6.7.17 to 12.7.17		Batt in rest. Carried out training in Rapid wiring, Raids, Lewis Gun, Bombing, Rifle	
			Grenades & Company & Platoon Drill. Four platoons daily were supplied for	#S.J
			work at SAPIGNIES & BEHAGNES watch points. Moved C Camp from H5d 2.6.6.	
			H5d 4.3. Batt bathed twice.	
BEUGNATRE	13.7.17	9.15pm	Batt left "C" Camp & marched into the line at R1. LAGNICOURT SECTOR.	#S.J
		11am	relieving the 2/6 WEST YORKSHIRE REGT. A & D Coys held the front line & posts	
			from left to Right respectively C & B in Support & Holding Main Line Resistance.	
LAGNICOURT	14.7.17 to 16.7.17	2pm & 4pm	Batt holding the line as on 13.7.17. Employed in deepening & back broading M.L.R.	#S.J
		10.2am	& wiring posts. During this period D Coy had one casualty 16.7.17, other coys nil.	
LAGNICOURT	17.7.17 to 21.7.17	10.30pm	A & D Coys were relieved from posts by C & B Coys. Batt employed in deepening	#S.J
			& widening & Back broading M.L.R & wiring posts. A Coy had 2 casualties C3 post	
			Killed 1 Wounded 1. D Coy had 3 killed & one wounded on 19.7.17 whilst working	

WAR DIARY 2/5 D.O.W. July 1917. Cont;

Army Form C. 2118.

Place	Date	Hour	Summary of Events and Information	Remarks and references to Appendices
LAGNICOURT	17.7.17 to 21.7.17 Continued		in B2 posn for B Coy. Batt relieved on the 21.7.17 by 2/4 D.O.W & marched into Reserve at VAULX. Relief complete 12.45 A.M.	A/S
VAULX	22.7.17 to 25.7.17		Batt in RESERVE. Rested during day. Found 4 platoons daily for work on trenches in R2 LAGNICOURT SECTOR from 10.0 P.M. to 2.0 A.M. Batt held 3 Lewis Gun posts in 2ⁿᵈ LINE of DEFENCE & one burial post in BOIS DE VAULX. Relieved on 25.7.17 by 1/6 D.o.W & went into Support in SUNKEN Rᵈ. N-S of LAGNICOURT. Lᵗ Col Major Brook from Batt and 2ⁿᵈ in command 1/c Major FAUDER.	A/S
LAGNICOURT	26.7.17 to 29.7.17		Batt in Support. Found working parties 60 for Dug outs in R2 SECTOR 9.60 for Dug outs in R1 Section working in 8 hr shifts at 10 pm. 6 am & 2 pm. C & A Coys & H.Q. were in Sunken Rd S of LAGNICOURT B & D Coys in Rd N of LAGNICOURT. Batt Relieved on 29.7.17 by 2/4 Koyli. Confirmation service by Archbishop of York.	A/S
BEUGNATRE	30.7.17 to 31.7.17		Batt in Rest at Camp H. S.D.4.3. Carried out Interior Economy, Bathing & Training	A/S

J.D.Best. L'Col.
2/5 Duke of Wellington's Regt

ORIGINAL

SECRET

WAR DIARY

of

2/5th Bn. DUKE OF WELLINGTON'S RGT.

PERIOD :- 1st to 31st AUGUST 1917.

VOLUME VIII

L Brook Major
for Lieut. Colonel
Commanding 2/5 Duke of Wellington's Regt.

WAR DIARY 1/5 Duke of Wellington's Regt.

or

INTELLIGENCE SUMMARY.

August /17

Army Form C. 2118.

Place	Date	Hour	Summary of Events and Information	Remarks and references to Appendices
BEUGNATRE	1.8.17 to 3.8.17	—	Battalion in "C" Camp. Training in platoon & coy drill & Lewis Gun, Bombing & Rifle Grenade. Rapid wiring & musketry. One platoon working party at GOMMECOURT & one platoon working party at SAPIGNIES per day. Interior economy preparing for the line.	#.S.J.
BEUGNATRE	4.8.17	9am to 4pm	6.15 PM Battalion marched into the line at NOREUIL LEFT Brigade Sub File relieve 4th West Yorkshire Regt, relief complete 1.0AM. No casualties. B coy left, D coy left Centre, A coy Rt Centre & C coy Right.	#.S.J.
NOREUIL	5.8.17 to 8.8.17	—	Battalion holding the line, carried out wiring in front of trenches at night and improving trenches by day. Established two new posts in trench approximately h.29.b.55.7 & 29 & b.28. On the 8.8.17 trenches were strafed with enemy trench mortars & movement was seen in front, the S.O.S was sent up but no attack developed. Casualties 2 killed 9 2 wounded. N° 241638 Pte Shearsmith 9 Kent Black died. Patrol work and found a German post.	#.S.J.
NOREUIL	9.8.17 4.0 AM		German post found by our patrol on the 6.8.17 was strafed by rifle grenades under supervision of Lieut Black and his Lewis Gun. One German killed by sniper.	#.S.J.
	8	11.0 PM	Battalion relieved by 4th Batt of Wellingtons Regt to go into support, owing to the wet state of the trenches relief not complete until 2.30 AM. Capt G BEAUMONT transferred to 1/5 York & Lanc's to take over 2nd in Command. Total Casualties 3 killed & 2 wounded.	

WAR DIARY

1/5-Duke of Wellingtons Regt Army Form C. 2118.

or

INTELLIGENCE SUMMARY.

Aug 1/17 continued

(Erase heading not required.)

Place	Date	Hour	Summary of Events and Information	Remarks and references to Appendices
NOREUIL	10.8.17 to 13.8.17	—	Battalion in Support at Depys at IGGAREE CORNERS & some Coys in JOINT TRENCH. H.Q. at VRAUCOURT. Two Gun posts Lewis, 2nd Line of Defence in front of VRAUCOURT. Battalion employed daily in working parties by day in burying & laying cables & in clearing trenches in LEFT & RIGHT NOREUIL SECTORS. One casualty in JOINT TRENCH by stray bullet on 13th.	W.S.J
BEUGNATRE	14.8.17 to 15.8.17	—	Battalion Bathing & training in Coy drill & Lewis Gun, Bombing & Rifle Grenades.	W.S.J
BEUGNATRE	16.8.17	—	Battalion moved out of tents in C Camp into Nissen huts in "C" Camp BEUGNATRE.	W.S.J
BEUGNATRE	17.8.17 19.8.17	—	Improved new Camp. Bathing, Church parade, Corps Horse show held at BIHUCOURT on 18.8.17. Lieuts BOWER, SYKES, ROBINSON & STEAD joined the Battalion on 19.8.17.	W.S.J
BEUGNATRE	20.8.17	10 p.m 10.40 p.m	Interior Economy preparing to go into line. Relieved in "C" Camp by 1/6 WEST YORKS Regt & relieved 1/5 West Yorks Regt in the line at BULLECOURT LEFT Bath. Sector, relief complete 12.30 A.M. No casualties. C Coy on Left front & B Coy in Reform, D Coy Left Support & A Coy Rt Support	W.S.J
BULLECOURT	21.8.17 to 24.8.17	—	Batt holding the line. Carried out wiring at night and improved trenches, deepened & cleared CHINA LANE. No. 241638 Pte Shepworth D Coy awarded Military Medal for making 22.8.17 successful patrol reconnaissance. A Coy relieved on night of 24/25th. No casualties.	W.S.J

WAR DIARY 1/5 Duke of Wellingtons Regt

INTELLIGENCE SUMMARY. August 1917 Continued.

Army Form C. 2118.

(Erase heading not required.)

Place	Date	Hour	Summary of Events and Information	Remarks and references to Appendices
BULLECOURT	25.8.17 to 28.8.17		Battalion in the line. Carried out wiring and clearing trenches of dead and water. Lt Col But DSO went to Brigade on 25.8.17 as Brigade Commander. Major F Brook took command of Battalion. Battalion relieved by the 1/4th Duke of Wellington Regt on night of 28/29 & went into reserve with Headquarters at MORY, two Coys at L'HOMME MORT, one at ECOUST and one at VRAUCOURT. Casualties during time 2 wounded 26.8.17. Died A. Coy.	H.S.J.
MORY	29.8.17 to 31.8.17		Battalion in reserve. Coy at L'Hd 30.8.17. Employed in working parties at night. one H.S.J. Coy on wire in front of second line defence at VRAUCOURT. one on communication trench (BULLECOURT AVENUE) and two Coys digging TIGER TRENCH.	

F Brook Major.
Comdg. 1/5 Batt Duke of Wellingtons Regt.

WAR DIARY
of
2/5TH BN. DUKE OF WELLINGTON'S REGIMENT

From 1st September 1917
To. 30th September 1917.

Volume 9

H.S. Jackson Lieut + A/tg
for Major
2/5th Duke of Wellington's Regt

WAR DIARY
INTELLIGENCE SUMMARY

Army Form C. 2118.

2/5 Duke of Wellington's Regt.
September 1917.

Place	Date	Hour	Summary of Events and Information	Remarks and references to Appendices
MORY	1.9.17, 2.9.17, 3.9.17, 4.9.17		Batt in reserve to Left Divisional Sector (BULLECOURT) Employed in working parties, 100 men unloading at R.E. dump E cost, remainder working on TIGER TRENCH. Occupied posts at URAUCOURT & Embankment at E cost ST.	H.S.
MORY	5.9.17		Relieved from Reserve by 7/4 YORK & LANES. Relieved 7/4 KOYLI in No 7 Camp.	H.S.
BEUGNATRE	6.9.17, 7–12.9.17		Battalion in Rest. Carried out training in Company drill, Lewis gun, Signalling. 1 officer & 20 other Ranks on working party at VAULX daily	H.S.
NOREUIL	13.9.17		Relieved 2/5 West Yorks Regt in Right Divisional Sector.	H.S.
NOREUIL	14.9.17		Batt holding the line. Worked on posts & wire at night. 2 Lieut JACK & 2 Lieut STEAD took out patrol to reconnoitre Road running through 4.30 A & C. No enemy seen.	H.S.
NOREUIL	15.9.17		Commenced work on Tramways & roadways in front of Nos 7, 18 & 19 posts.	H.S.
NOREUIL	16.9.17		Patrols went out under Capt. Horton. D/s reconnaissance met in T X Roads about Q.6 Central. 5.4 N.W. Enemy not obtained. Patrols returned without casualties.	H.S.
NOREUIL	18.9.17, 19.9.17, 20.9.17		Mutual Yineets Sy Ka, Borzay, Black & Jack took part in the above patrol.	H.S.
NOREUIL	21.9.17		Relieved by the 2/4 Duke of Wellington to go into Support at HOBART CROSS. Number of casualties during tour: 1 Killed 1/B Coy, 1 wounded A Coy (remainder working)	H.S.
NOREUIL	22–28.9.17		Batt in Support, employed on working parties daily	H.S.
NOREUIL	29.9.17		Battalion relieved by 2 Coys 7/4 YORK & LANES, 2 Coys 2/5 KOYLI marched to No 7 Camp	H.S.
BEUGNATRE	30.9.17		Batt in rest. Bathed & inferior Economy. Major Brook took charge of Batt.	H.S.

J Brook Major

SECRET

Original

Vol 10

3 sheets

10 g.

WAR DIARY

OF

2/5TH. Bn. DUKE OF WELLINGTON'S REGIMENT

FROM 1st OCTOBER 1917
TO 31st OCTOBER 1917.

[signature] Lieut-Colonel.
Commdg. 2/5th Bn. Duke of Wellington's Regiment.

VOLUME 10.

WAR DIARY
INTELLIGENCE SUMMARY.
(Erase heading not required.)

Army Form C. 2118.

2/5 Bn. Wellington Regt.

October 1917.

Place	Date	Hour	Summary of Events and Information	Remarks and references to Appendices
BEUGNATRE	1/10/17 to 6/10/17	-	Battalion in Brigade rest. Carried out training in Company drill, forming up for attack. Attack practice & Lewis Gun, Bombing, Signalling & Rifle Grenade training.	H.S.J.
BEUGNATRE	7/10/17	6.12 a.m. 6.0 p.m.	In trenches economy & preparing for the line. Marched into the line at NOREUIL & took over the centre Brigade section at the APEX. Relieving the 2/5 YORK & LANC'S Regt. No casualties during relief. Relief complete 11.30 p.m.	H.S.J.
NOREUIL	8/10/17 9/10/17		Holding the line with two Coys in the front line D & C Coys in support B & A Coys. Carried out work in improving the trenches and wiring. No casualties.	H.S.J.
NOREUIL	10/10/17	7.0 p.m.	Relieved by 13th KING'S LIVERPOOL Regt 3rd Division. Relief completed 11.30 p.m. A Coy had one casualty, wounded. Marched to No 7 Camp BEUGNATRE.	H.S.J.
BEUGNATRE	11/10/17	-	In trenches economy & preparing to vacate camp.	H.S.J.
BEUGNATRE	12/10/17	11.0 a.m.	Marched into Divisional Rest at BEULENCOURT.	H.S.J.
BEULENCOURT	13/10/17 14/10/17		Battalion in rest. Re-equipping. Reorganisation of Coys and platoons for new method of attack & Church parade.	H.S.J.
BEULENCOURT	15/10/17 to 21/10/17	9-12.30 2 p.m-4.30	Platoon, Coy & Battalion training in the attack & forming up on tape line. Training in Lewis Gun, Bombing, Rifle Grenade & Signalling. Church parade. Severe lecture by the D.A.C.G.	H.S.J.
BEULENCOURT	22/10/17 to 28/10/17		Coy, Battalion & Brigade practise in the attack & forming up on tape line. Lecture by Platoon Drill Officers. Yarnbling on a compass bearing at night & lecture by G.O.C. % Divisional Signal Coy on communications. Church parade.	H.S.J.

Army Form C. 2118.

WAR DIARY
or
INTELLIGENCE SUMMARY.

H.S. Duke of Wellington's Regt.

October 1917 Cont

(Erase heading not required.)

Instructions regarding War Diaries and Intelligence Summaries are contained in F. S. Regs., Part II. and the Staff Manual respectively. Title pages will be prepared in manuscript.

Place	Date	Hour	Summary of Events and Information	Remarks and references to Appendices
BEAULENCOURT	19.10.17	—	Platoon training & cleaning camp preparing for move.	A.S.J
BEAULENCOURT	20.10.17	7.35AM	Battalion moved to COURCELLES on route for GOUY. arrived COURCELLES LE COMPTE 11·30AM. No men fell out on march.	A.S.J
COURCELLES	21.10.17	8·5AM	Battalion moved to GOUY, arrived GOUY 2·0PM. One man fell out on march. Billeted in farms & private billets.	A.S.J

T. B. Best Lt Col.
Duke of Wellington's Regt.

2/5 Duke of Wellington's Regt.

Secret.

10 sheets

WAR DIARY
OF
2/5th. Bn. Duke of Wellington's Regt.

From :- 1st November 1917
To :- 30th   "   "

Volume II.

J Brook
Lieut. Colonel.
Commdg. 2/5th Bn. Duke of Wellington's Regt.

WAR DIARY
INTELLIGENCE SUMMARY

1/5 Duke of Wellingtons
November, 1917

Army Form C. 2118.

Place	Date	Hour	Summary of Events and Information	Remarks and references to Appendices
GOUY	1.11.17	—	Interior economy, Straightening up of billets by & platoon training.	#.S.J.
	6.11.17	—	Lewis guns on range.	
GOUY	7.11.17	—	Training of Lewis Gunners, Signallers, Bombers, Officers and Platoon Sergts went to see demonstration of attack with tanks at WAILLY	#.S.J.
GOUY	8.11.17	—	Batt went to WAILLY by Lorries to practise attack with tanks	#.S.J.
GOUY	9.11.17	—	Batt took part in Brigade scheme for practising communication with Contact Aeroplane	#.S.J.
GOUY	10.11.17 11.11.17	—	Practising an attack through ground formed up behind tanks by Coys.	#.S.J.
GOUY	12.11.17	9.30 AM	Battalion inspected by new Brigade Commander. 10.0 AM Battalion training informing up behind tanks and advancing to attack.	#.S.J.
GOUY	13.11.17	—	Interior economy, preparing to move. 6.55 pm Battalion marched to ACHIET LE PETIT, arrived 12.45 pm.	#.S.J.
ACHIET LE PETIT	14.11.17	—	Interior economy & Battalion training in the attack.	#.S.J.
	15.11.17 16.11.17	7.30 AM	Battalion marched to LECHELLE	
LECHELLE	17.11.17 to 18.11.17	4.30 PM	Interior economy & fitting out with bombs. 19.11.17. Officers went up to inspect the line at HAVRINCOURT WOOD. Battalion marched to Billets in BERTINCOURT.	#.S.J.
BERTINCOURT	19.11.17	—	Battalion having previous to the attack	
BERTINCOURT	20.11.17	6.30 AM 9.15 AM	Battalion marched to the assembly position for attack at PLACE MORT HOMME, HAVRINCOURT WOOD. Battalion moved forward to form up, marched in column towards HAVRINCOURT and on approaching CHATEAU WOOD came under machine gun & rifle fire. At this point the Commanding Officer Lieut Col T.D. Best D.S.O. & Lieut Rockell were killed & Lieuts J.A. HAIGH & W. THOMAS wounded. 9.26 Casualties 2 Oth. Ranks sustained	#.S.J.

WAR DIARY

1st Batt. Wellington Regt.

Nov 1917 Cont.

INTELLIGENCE SUMMARY

Army Form C. 2118.

Place	Date	Hour	Summary of Events and Information	Remarks and references to Appendices
BERTINCOURT	20-11-17 Continued	—	Capt. & Adjt. H.S. batten took command of the Battalion at this point & handed over to Capt F. Sykes on reaching the Brown Line. The enemy opposition consisted of snipers & a strong point. This was attacked by D Coy under Capt. T. Goodale. 1 offr. & 58 other Ranks & 2 machine guns captured & a L.P.O. intelligence officer & a N.C.O rescued. The Battalion then reorganised and continued the advance in lines of sections to take up its position on the forming up line. On approaching this line the Batt. came under heavy M.G. & Rifle fire from R & D 15. A platoon was sent forward under Lieut Black to deal with it & on approaching, found a tank ditched near the strong point & being bombed furiously by the enemy. Capt. Macon (who had gone forward with the tank) & tank commander & crew were defending the tank from the outside. The platoon worked round the posts rear, killing 5 & capturing 3, the remainder of the garrison ran away towards GRAINCOURT. They were engaged under Lewis Gun fire at R4 d 9 6 & heavy casualties inflicted. The Battalion was then reorganised on the forming up line & with tanks attacked the objective. KANGAROO ALLEY was captured & occupied by D Coy. A strong point at LOCK No 6 was captured by C Coy & 2 offrs & 64 other Ranks taken prisoners, the remainder of the garrison would not leave the dug out so a P Bomb was thrown in & the dug out set on fire. A strong point at E 2 8 6.4. was also captured by Lieut Black & Platoon, 2 officers, 59 other Ranks & 2 machine guns being captured. A 139 C Coy then pushed forward through D & continued the advance across the BAPAUME-CAMBRAI ROAD until the final objective for the day was captured. A platoon under Lieut Enever captured a strong point took 2 M.G's, 2 officers & 20 other Ranks prisoners. The position was consolidated & held with 13 on the R. & flank with a defensive	

WAR DIARY

Army Form C. 2118.

1/5 Battn. of Wellington's Regt.
Nov 1917 Continued.

INTELLIGENCE SUMMARY

(Erase heading not required.)

Place	Date	Hour	Summary of Events and Information	Remarks and references to Appendices
BERTINCOURT	20-11-17 Continued	—	Attack down the HINDENBURG SUPPORT LINE. A Coy in the centre & C Coy on the left in touch with the 36th Division on the Canal Bank. D coy occupying KANGAROO ALLEY in Support. Batt: H.Q. in KANGAROO ALLEY. During the day the Battalion Captured 353 prisoners, 15 machine Guns & 1 Trench Mortar. Total number of casualties. Killed Lt Col Best D.S.O. Lieut J.G. Bolden. Lieut JAMES HAIGH, died of wounds Lts JT & Z Thomas wounded, 10 other Ranks killed, 3 O/Rs wounded & 4 other Rks missing.	HS
KANGAROO ALLEY N.W. GRAINCOURT	2-11-17	6AM 10.0 AM	Major F. Brook arrived and took command of the Battalion. 1/5 Battalion formed up for attack with tanks, 40 tanks arrived. The enemy were too alert for a frontal attack to be made. B,A & C coys bombed up the HINDENBURG SUPPORT LINE in E22A&C. Reyamounted as far as E22A55 when they were held up by a strong point. A Platoon of A coy under Lieut Ridgway rushed the strong point & captured it, taking 40 prisoners. Lieut Ridgway was killed & Capt Hurson wounded. The position of A,B & C were now, A in the Sunken Road at E16D22, B in trench at E22A72, & C in Trench with tank at E22A54. The enemy received strong reinforcements from the direction of MOEUVRES & rendered further progress impossible. At 3.30 pm the Rely Capt H.S Jackson secured the arrival of a tank which had lost direction & returned it and conducted it to the point where the Battalion was held up. D coy was then pushed forward & all coys with the assistance of the tank attacked and captured the enemy trench system as far as E21C57 & E21C60.01. The Position was consolidated and the tank proceeded forward. Lieut Cain rd the A Coy Left Centre, B Coy Right Centre & D Coy Right. The final objective & came in contact with a strongly enemy	

WAR DIARY or INTELLIGENCE SUMMARY

Army Form C. 2118.

4/5 D. of W. Regt.
Nov 1917. Cont.

Place	Date	Hour	Summary of Events and Information	Remarks and references to Appendices
RANGAROO ALLEY	21-11-17	—	Counter attack estimated strong the 2 Battalions. The attack was temporarily broken up & the tank returned twice at 4.15 p.m. At 5.0 p.m. the enemy strongly counter-attacked our position but was driven off by Lewis Gun & rifle fire. At midnight the Batt. was relieved by the 1/6 WEST YORKSHIRE REGT & marched into support in the HINDENBURG LINE at KILBY D. Prisoners captured 70 & 2 Machine Guns. Casualties. Lieut Ridgway Killed. Capt Thrower wounded. 6 ORs Killed & 9 ORs wounded.	A.S. J
N.W. GRAINCOURT Continued				
HINDENBURG LINE KILB.D	22-11-17	—	The Battalion remained in support until 10 p.m. when it marched into trenches in HAURINCOURT WOOD.	A.S. J
HAURINCOURT WOOD	23-11-17	—	Battalion marched into billets at BERTINCOURT, arrived 2.0 p.m.	A.S. J
BERTINCOURT	24-11-17 to 25-11-17	—	Battalion in rest. Carried out Interior Economy & cleaning equipment. Lieut Col Best D.S.O. & Lieut Bodley billeted in the British Cemetery RUYAULCOURT.	A.S. J
SUNKEN RD. N.W. ANNEUX	26-11-17	1.30 p.m. 11.0 a.m.	Batt. marched into support in Sunken Road N.W. ANNEUX. 2/Lieut LIDDLE and 4 ORs wounded. Battalion in support. 7.30 p.m. moved to take over the line in BOURLON WOOD from the 4/ D of W Regt & prepare for attack on the following day.	A.S. J
BOURLON WOOD	27-11-17	6.20 a.m.	Battalion attacked in pitchy darkness. Dispositions were as follows. B on Right A Centre C on Left & D in support. C coy advanced to the outskirts of BOURLON WOOD & S.E. side of Village. D coy advanced to Slag X Roads at Fr D.3.4. A & B Coys were held up after going 50 yds by a nest of Machine Guns in a strong point at approximately F.8.5.4. the undergrowth was very thick & no further progress was made. The ground on our Right was	A.S. J

(A7092). Wt. W12839/M1293. 753,000. 1/17. D.D. & L., Ltd. Forms/C.2118"14.

WAR DIARY
INTELLIGENCE SUMMARY

1/5 Bank of Wellington Regt. Army Form C. 2118.

Nov 1917 Cont.

Place	Date	Hour	Summary of Events and Information	Remarks and references to Appendices
BOURLON WOOD	27.11.17 Cont.		also held up & had to withdraw to their former position. These positions were held until 4.0 p.m. against several strong enemy attacks. At 4.30 p.m. a complete line was formed & touch gained with the 1/6 Duke of Wellingtons on our left at F4 b 6.5, though the slow Cross Roads at F4 a 2.9 to F4 a 7.9 to touch with the Irish Guards. During the day 12 prisoners were taken & the following casualties sustained. Killed 2nd Lieut. W.S. Down. 2nd Lieut. Groves (died of wounds). Heavy 2nd Lieut. Melville. Wounded Capt. F. Sykes Capt. W. Potterton, Rev. A.B. Wright C.F. Lieut Edwards, Lieut P. Black, Lieut Q. S. just 2nd Lieut Abrams. 18 other Ranks killed. 14. missing 144. wounded. At 11 p.m. the Battn was relieved by 2 Coys of Dismounted Cavalry and moved back to support in BOURLON WOOD approx F13 D.	H.S.J
BOURLON WOOD	28.11.17		Battalion in Support. At 6.0 p.m. Batt had to stand to be ready to move forward to repel a counter attack, nothing serious developed. 7.0 p.m. Battalion was relieved & went into reserve in the HINDENBURG SUPPORT LINE at K9 C.	H.S.J
HINDENBURG LINE K9C	29.11.17 to 30.11.17		Battalion in reserve, carried out cleaning of arms and equipment & replenishing ammunition & bombs. Batt stood to all day owing to a heavy German attack having developed S. of MOEUVRES. Brig. General Bradford V.C. M.C. killed by shell.	H.S.J

J. Bradford Lieut Col.

2/5TH. BN. DUKE OF WELLINGTON'S REGIMENT.   War Diary
OPERATION ORDERS   BY   LT-COL. F.A.D. BEST, D.S.O.
         COMMANDING
                        NOVEMBER 17th 1917.

                                    Copy No. 24

1. The 62nd Division will attack on Z day, objectives, 1st the BLUE Line, 2nd the BROWN Line and 3rd the RED Line as already marked on maps issued to Coys. The 185th Brigade on the right, and 187th Brigade on the left will capture the BLUE and BROWN Line and the 186th Brigade will leapfrog through and capture the RED Line. Dispositions of the Brigade being as shewn in Priliminary Instruction Scheme "A" already issued.
The 51st Division on our right will be attacking CANTAING and the 36th Division the trenches to the West of CANAL-DU-NORD South of the CAMBRAI-BAPAUME Road. At the same time demonstrations will be made against the enemy's lines S. & S.W. of MOEUVRES and their trenches there kept under heavy Artillery fire.

2. BATTALION OBJECTIVE The Battalion will clear and capture the area K.4.d.1.5. - E.22.c.9.2 - E.26.d.9.5 - K.3.d.45.00 bounded on the right by the HINDENBURG SUPPORT LINE (allotted to the 2/7th. Bn. D.of W. Regt.) and on the left by the CANAL-DU-NORD. Intermediate objective KANGAROO ALLEY TRENCH.
General True Bearing of the advance will be 343°.

3. Hour of Brigade Zero will be notified later.

4. METHOD OF ATTACK. At Brigade Zero minus   the Battalion will move from the assembly position East of HAVRINCOURT in column of route, 100 yards between Platoons and 150 yards between Coys. Order of march "D" "B" "C" "A" proceeding via road from K.21.d.5.5 K.15.b.5.2 to K.9.b.5.2., from this point Coys. will branch off to the positions of assembly for attack. The leading wave being assembled in the GRAINCOURT-DEMICOURT Sunken Road, which is the Jumping off line for the Battalion.
"D" Coy. in line of sections will move across the whole front and capture KANGAROO ALLEY. It will be assisted by one platoon of "A" Coy moving on its left along the CANAL BANK in two lines of sections, this platoon of "A" Coy. will be responsible for protecting the left flank of KANGAROO ALLEY from the CANAL. At least 5 Strong points will be constructed in KANGAROO ALLEY as soon as possible and O.C. "D" Coy. will assist the advance of the Coys. passing through his, with covering fire, if required. Particular attention must be paid to the M.G. positions in trench running South from centre of KANGAROO ALLEY.
"B" & "C" Coys. will follow "D" Coy. at 100 yards distance in two lines in line of sections, two platoons each in the front line and one platoon each in the 2nd line, distance of 150 yards between lines.
"B" Coy. will clear all the area East of the Communication Trench running from E.27.b.5.5 to E.28.c.1.2 exclusive of above C.T. Particular attention will be paid to the M.G's in SAPS from HINDENBURG LINE in E. 28. b & d. these should be dealt with by 2/7th.D.of W. Regt. working on right, but this must not be taken for granted. "B" Coy. must be prepared to throw back a defensive flank in the event of the failure of the Unit on its right, and in any case will take special precautions for the safety of this flank.
"C" Coy. will clear area West of Communication Trench (inclusive) mentioned in "B" Coys. instructions and will be assisted by one platoon of "A" Coy., advancing with C's leading line and hugging the CANAL BANK. This platoon will be responsible for protecting the left flank from attack and will take up positions along the CANAL BANK and in the trenches just S.E. of crossing of BAPAUME-CAMBRAI Road and CANAL. "C" Coy. will establish a Block 80 yards up CANAL TRENCH and also a strong battle patrol at cross Roads E.27.b.6.7.
"A" Coy. less two platoons, will remain in reserve along the CANAL BANK at K.3.b.0.2 and will consolidate against the CANAL BANK protecting the left flank. O.C. "A" Coy. will be responsible for protecting the left flank of the area from attack west of CANAL-DU-NORD.

4. (cont'd)

LINE TO BE CONSOLIDATED. The trench running 250 yards North of BAPAUME-CAMBRAI Road will be consolidated by "B" & "C" Coys. and will be held at all costs. "D" Coy. will as detailed before construct 5 Strong points in KANGAROO ALLEY.

TANKS. All surviving Tanks from the 187th Brigade attack will co-operate in the Brigade attack but will move forward to the areas to be cleared, without waiting for the Infantry. At least two Tanks will be specially detailed to hug the CANAL BANK and deal with resistance there. The Infantry will not wait for the Tanks, but must push on by themselves.

ARTILLERY. There will be no Artillery barrage after Brigade Zero hour except in GRAINCOURT where it will continue till Zero plus 30 minutes. Special Artillery co-operation will be provided for the trenches West of the CANAL-DU-NORD. Detailed Instructions of this will be issued later.

Machine Gun Barrage as detailed in Scheme "A".
Two Machine Guns will be allotted to the Battalion during the attack, and will cover the attack in KANGAROO ALLEY from about K.4.d.0.4. One Gun eventually pushing forward on the capture of the final objective to about E.27.b.3.0 and the other remaining where it can protect the right flank of the Battalion from direction of BOURLON.

CONTACT AEROPLANES. Times will be notified later.

COMMUNICATIONS. Battalion Headquarters from after commencing our attack will be at cross Roads K.9.b.6.2. until capture of final objective when it will move to E.28.d.4.5. In the first case "B" & "C" Coys will form a joint Runners post at Communication Trench on right of "C" Coys. front at E.27.b.4.5 which will carry to "D" Coys. post at E.27.d.9.0. "D" Coy. will transmit to K.4.c.5.4. which will be Battalion Relay post.
Visual communication will be established between Coys. and with Battalion Headquarters Relay post. "B" & "C" Joint station would require to be about E.27.d.5.7.

REGIMENTAL AID POST at Battalion Headquarters and will move to new Battalion Headquarters when latter moves forward.

PRISONERS will be sent to Battalion Headquarters with an escort of not more than 5%, slightly wounded men should be utilised for this purpose whenever possible.

WATCHES to be synchronised at 12 noon, 5 p.m. and 10 p.m. on Y day.

ARMS & EQUIPMENT. All walking wounded must bring back their Arms and Equipment with them, ammunition should be collected from them before returning. No unwounded man except a S.B. will accompany a wounded man back. Anyone doing so will be treated as a straggler.

H.S. Jackson
Capt. & Adjt.
2/5th.Bn. Duke of Wellington's Regiment.

Copies to:-
Nos. 1 to 4.	O.C. "A" Coy.
5 " 8	" "B" Coy.
9 " 12	" "C" Coy.
13 " 16	" "D" Coy.
17	Sig. Officer.
18	2/7th.D.of.W.Regt.
19	2/6th. D.of.W. Regt.
20	Bde. Hqrs.
21	Office copy.
22	Transport Officer.
23	Lieut. Bodker.
24	War Diary.
25	Medical Officer.

2/5TH. BN. DUKE OF WELLINGTON'S REGIMENT.
OPERATION ORDERS BY MAJOR F. BROOK.
COMMANDING 21st November 1917.
------

1. The 186th Brigade will attack at 10 a.m., 2/5th.D.of.W. Regt. operating on the left and the 2/7th.D.of.W.Regt. on the centre.

2. The Battalion objective will be the HINDENBURG SUPPORT LINE in E.22 and E.21.b. and then the line running from Crucifix in E.17.a. to Sunken Road at E.15.d.4.5.

3. Method of attack. No Tanks have arrived so the HINDENBURG SUPPORT LINE will be attacked from the junction of trench at E.22.c.95.25. "A" Coy. will lead the attack along the front support trench, "B" Coy. will mop up rear support trench, "C" Coy. will work in support to "A" Coy, "D" Coy. will remain in reserve in the trench from E.28.a.0.7 to E.22.c.9.1.
When the HINDENBURG SUPPORT LINE has been cleared, Coys. will move across the open and advance to the final objective and take up the following poistions. "B" Coy. on right, "A" Coy. in centre, and "C" Coy. on the left. "C" Coy. will be responsible for guarding the left flank. "D" Coy. will move up into the HINDENBURG SUPPORT LINE in support.

4. Battalion Headquarters will be at E.28.a.2.8. and as the attack proceeds will move to E.22.d.0.1.

5. Machine Guns. 2 Machine guns are attached to the Battalion.

6. Orders regarding Prisoners, Arms & Equipment etc. the same as in orders for the 20th Nov.1917.

Major.
Commandg. 2/5th.Bn.Duke of Wellington's

2/5TH. BN. DUKE OF WELLINGTON'S REGIMENT.
OPERATION ORDERS BY MAJOR F.BROCK.
COMMANDING
November 26th. 1917.
- - - - - - - -

1. The 186th Brigade will attack BOURLON WOOD and RAILWAY on the morning of the 27th. The 187th Brigade will operate on the left and the Guards Division will operate on the right.

2. Battalion Objective the line of RAILWAY F.1.d.1.0 to F.1.c.2.7.

3. Zero Hour is 6.20 a.m.

4. The Battalion will retire from the Posts and form up half an hour before Zero along the road running E. and W. from F.7.c.b. "B" Coy. on the right, "C" Coy. on the left "A" Coy in the centre and "D" Coy. in rear of "A" Coy. "B" & "C" Coys. will clear the Wood to the Northern edge, "A" Coy. will pass through this Coy. and establish a line along the road in F.7.b. "D" Coy. will pass right through and form a line of Posts at final objective. Main line of defence will be formed along line of "A" Coys. objective.

5. Artillery. There will be an Artillery barrage on enemy front posts for Zero plus 10 minutes, after this the barrage will advance at the rate of 100 yards in 5 minutes and will continue until Zero plus 50 minutes. It will then drop to a light protective fire.

6. Machine guns. 2 Machine guns will be attached to the Battalion in the attack and will be under the direction of the Commanding Officer.

7. Stokes Guns. 2 Stokes Guns are under the command of this Unit.

8. Battalion Headquarters and Regimental Aid post will be at the

8. (cont'd) Chalet, BOURLON WOOD.

9. Orders relating to Prisoners, Arms & Equipment etc. will be same as in orders for the 20th Nov. 1917.

F. Brook.
Major.
Commandg. 2/5th.Bn. Duke of Wellington's Regiment.

<u>Secret.</u>

ORIGINAL

War Diary.
of
2/5th Bn. Duke of Wellington's Regt.
From 1st Dec. 1917
To 31st Dec. 1917

Volume 12.

Major
Commdg. 2/5th Duke of Wellington's Rgt.

Original

WAR DIARY December 1917

Army Form C. 2118.

INTELLIGENCE SUMMARY. 1/5 Duke of Wellington Regt.

(Erase heading not required.)

Vol 12

Place	Date	Hour	Summary of Events and Information	Remarks and references to Appendices
HINDENBURG LINE R&D	1.12.17	—	Battalion in support. 6.0 p.m. moved into positions in the HINDENBURG LINE at R1 & R3 A to consolidate the line and held it as a defensive position in case of attack.	H.S.J.
HINDENBURG LINE R&D	2.12.17	—	Battalion holding the line. Casualties in the line nil. At transport lines HERMES 5 wounded	H.S.J.
LEBUCQUIERE	3.12.17	11.0 P.M.	Relieved by the 1/4th Royal Fusiliers and marched into Reserve at LEBUCQUIERE. 1 man killed & 1 wounded on route.	H.S.J.
	4.12.17	12.30 P.M.	Battalion marched to FREMICOURT to entrain for BEAUMETZ. Arrived BEAUMETZ 4.30 P.M. & then marched into Billets at BELLACOURT.	H.S.J.
BELLACOURT	5.12.17	2.0 P.M.	Battalion marched to HARBARCQ arrived 5.0 P.M.	H.S.J.
HARBARCQ	6.12.17	8.10 A.M.	Battalion marched to BAILLEUL AUX CORNAILLES arrived 1.0 P.M.	H.S.J.
BAILLEUL AUX CORNAILLES	7.12.17 to 10.12.17	—	Battalion noting & requisitioning, reequipment & cleaning of equipment	H.S.J.
	10.12.17	6.45 A.M.	Battalion marched to ANNEZIN VIA HOUDAIN, HAILLICOURT & FEUQUERILLE arrived 3.0 P.M.	
ANNEZIN	11.12.17	—	Requiping. Bathing. Training in Transport, Cooks under R.S.M., Lewis Gun, Bombing, Musketry & Signalling	H.S.J.
	14.12.17	9.45 A.M.	Battalion marched to CANTRAINE.	
CANTRAINE	15.12.17 to 18.12.17	8.0 A.M.	Battalion carried out training in Lewis Gun, Bombing, Sniping & Battalion Drill	H.S.J.
	18.12.17	8.0 A.M.	moved to ANNEZIN, arrived 11.30 A.M.	
ANNEZIN	19.12.17	8.15 A.M.	marched to BAILLEUL AUX CORNAILLES arrived 4.0 P.M. Had great trouble with transport owing to frost.	H.S.J.
BAILLEUL	20.12.17 to 24.12.17	—	Battalion carried out manual & specialist training. Military medals were awarded to the following for gallantry during the operations commencing 20/11/17 to 24/11/17. N° 12391 Sgt Beart E. N° 263029 Pte Lipton W.A. 240479 Sgt Eastwood H.R. 203949 Pte Yewlett S. 241689 Cpl Parker C.F. 25069 Cpl Coe Front J. 240981 L/Cpl Ellington. 241414 Sgt Prestly C. 241417 Pte Marsden W. 203206 Cpl Glatchly 235092 Pte Slade H. 240941 L/Cpl Halliwell J. 204403 Pte Applewood L. 240950 Sgt Mitchill R. 241663 Pte Simpson T. 240970 Cpl Slater T. 204804 Pte Sutcliffe P. 241087 Pte Sutcliffe F. 241049 Pte Thorp E. 265782 Pte Walker G.	H.S.J.

Original

WAR DIARY
INTELLIGENCE SUMMARY
(Erase heading not required.)

Army Form C. 2118.

December 1917. Cont.
1/5 Duke of Wellington Regt.

Instructions regarding War Diaries and Intelligence Summaries are contained in F. S. Regs., Part II. and the Staff Manual respectively. Title pages will be prepared in manuscript.

Place	Date	Hour	Summary of Events and Information	Remarks and references to Appendices
BAILLEUL	24/12/17 & 25	-	24603 Pte Marshall H. 25078 Pte Ellis W. 262639 Pte Gibbs W. 242897 L/Sgt Priestley H. (BAR to M.M.)	H.S.J.
BAILLEUL	25.12.17	-	Xmas day. Special dinners were given to the men & the rest of the day spent in entertainments.	H.S.J.
BAILLEUL	26.12.17 to 31.12.17	-	Battalion carrying out specialist training, manual & firing on Range. 30.12.17 Were working parties of 3 offs & 150 men & 10 ff. 240 men were out to the forward area to the 1/25 & 1/6 Lancashire Fusiliers respectively. 31.12.17. Major Goodall T. Capt H.S. Jackson. Capt E.S. Thrower were awarded the D.S.O. Lieut Black D, B/Cpt Burnang G.V. Lieut Harris E. Kent Jack A.S. Capt W. Roberson Rome Rees A.B. Wright the M.C. for gallantry in the operations commencing hour 20.11.1917.	H.S.J.

Tom Goodall Major
Commanding 2/5th Bn Duke of Wellington's Regt.

War Diary

of

2nd Bn. Duke of Wellington's Regt.

From January 1st 1918 to January 31st 1918

Volume 13.

Frank Kent-Ct.
O.E. 2/. Bn. Duke of Wellington's Regt.

ORIGINAL.

2/5 Duke of Wellingtons Regt Army Form C. 2118.

January 1918.

WAR DIARY
or
INTELLIGENCE SUMMARY.
(Erase heading not required.)

Place	Date	Hour	Summary of Events and Information	Remarks and references to Appendices
BAILLEUL	Jan 1st Jan 3.		Battalion training in Specialist subjects, manual & platoon in attack.	W.S.J.
BAILLEUL	4.1.18		Divisional General presented ribbon to officers & men of the Battalion who gained honours in the operations commencing Nov 20. LIEUT COL T.D. BEST late commanding 2nd (officers) was awarded a BAR to D.S.O., Major T. GOODALL D.S.O. was awarded the M.C. in NEW YEARS honours.	W.S.J.
BAILLEUL	5.1.18 8.1.11		Battalion training in Specialist subjects, manual & platoon attack. 8.1.18 No.240921 C.S.M. WILKINSON W.S. was awarded the D.C.M. in new year honours.	W.S.J.
BAILLEUL	9.1.18		Battalion moved in bivouac reserve at ST. AUBIN. Travelled by train from TINQUES to MAROEUL. Transport travelled by road.	W.S.J.
ST AUBIN	10.1.18 13.1.18		Battalion training in Lewis gun, Bombing & manual. 11.1.18. Brigade platoon competition held. Army Commander presented ribbons to men of the Battalion & inspected billets.	W.S.J.
ST AUBIN	14.1.18		Battalion relieved the 1/6th W.Y. Regt in the line A. front line B. Support, Co Dixnicour.	W.S.J.
OPPY	15.1.18		Trenches became unpassable owing to rain & thaw & considerable hardship was experienced	W.S.J.
OPPY	16.1.18		Patrol went out from Bradford post under 2/Lt FOREST to examine state of our wire & enemy trill post, no enemy was encountered.	
OPPY	17.1.18		Patrol under Lieut Steel was ordered to examine old trench running from Bradford	

ORIGINAL
WAR DIARY of 1/5 Duke of Wellington's Regt.
INTELLIGENCE SUMMARY
(Erase heading not required.)

January 1918. Cont:

Army Form C. 2118.

Place	Date	Hour	Summary of Events and Information	Remarks and references to Appendices
OPPY	18.1.18		Patrol towards enemy line, owing to unsatisfactory leadership the patrol did not get beyond our wire	H.S.J.
OPPY	19.1.18 20.1.18		Interdivisional relief took place. Relieving A & C Relieving B. Patrol under 2/Lt Forrest went out into no mans land to way lay enemy patrols, this patrol did not see any enemy. During the night 2/Lt Sykes & Mackenzie went out to reconnoitre, they lost direction & inadvertently reached the enemy wire. 2/Lt Mackenzie was shot 2/Lt Sykes severely wounded. By trench but succeeded in fighting his way clear & reached our line	H.S.J.
OPPY	21.1.18 22.1.18		Relieved from the line by the 4/5 K.O.Y.L.I & returned on the morning of the 23 to billets at ST AUBIN. Casualties during tour. 1 O/R missing believed killed. 1 O/R wounded. 2 O/Rs wounded	H.S.J
ST AUBIN	23.1.18 31.1.18		Battalion in reserve. Carried out training. Orders were received for the Battalion to be amalgamated with the 1/5 W.R. Regt. Amalgamation took place on the 31.1.18. Lt. Col Walker taking command. The no. of Battalion 5th West Riding Reg't.	H.S.J

Abbott Lieut Col

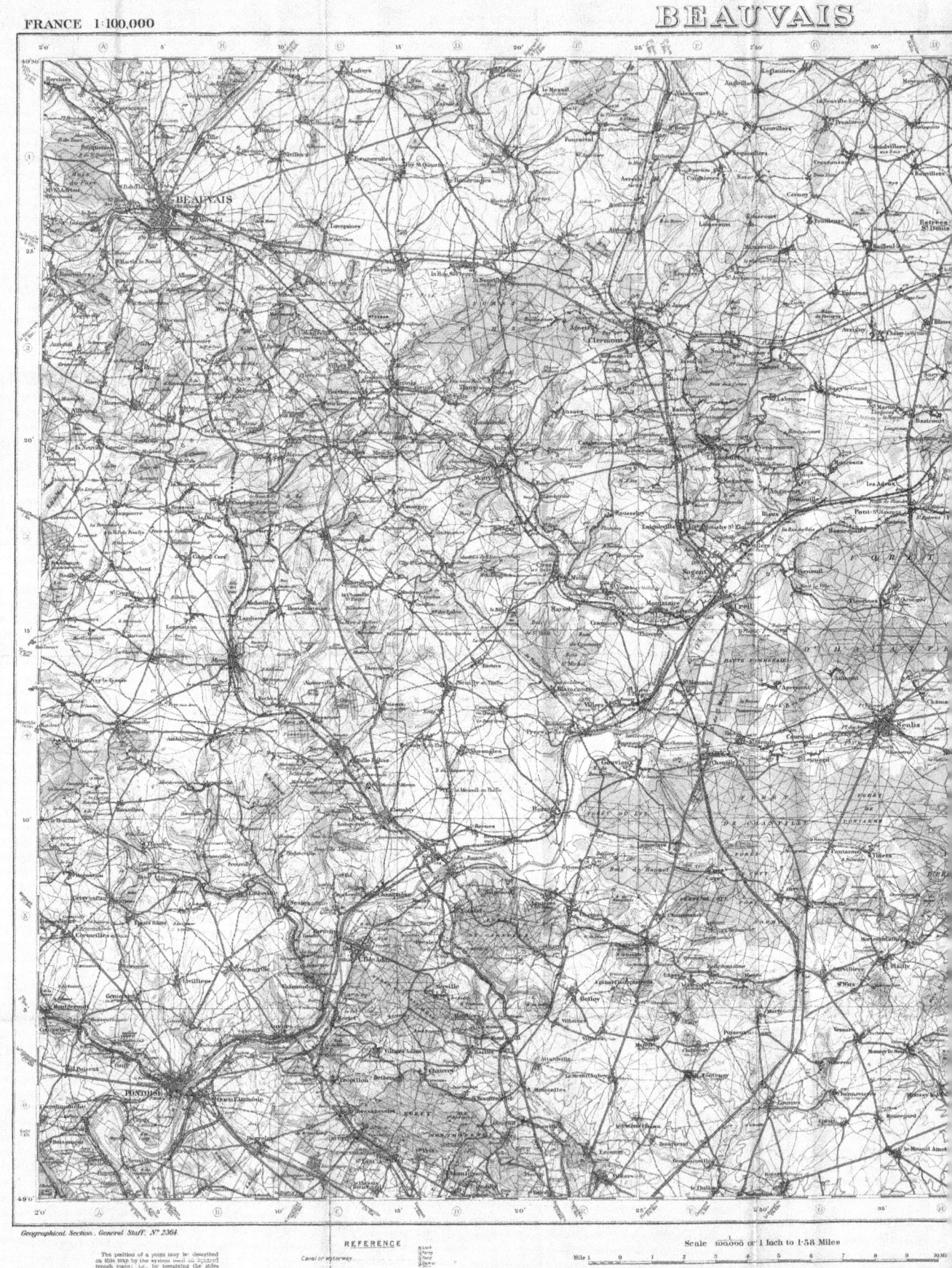

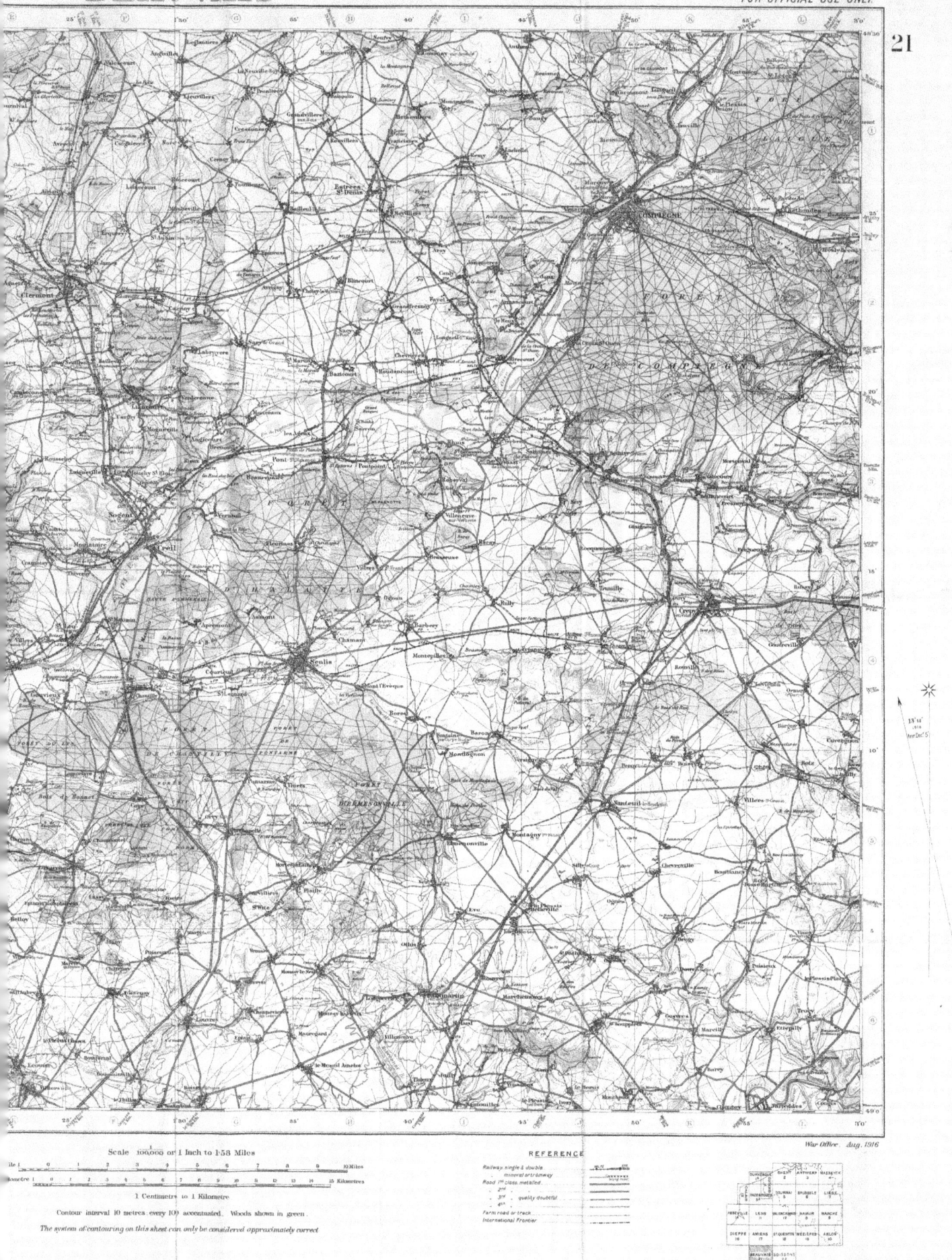

BEAUVAIS 21.

FRANCE.

Scale $\frac{1}{100,000}$

CALAIS 13	DUNKERQUE 1A	OSTEND 1	GHENT 2	ANTWERP 3	MAESEYCK 4
	HAZEBROUCK 5A		TOURNAI 5	BRUSSELS 6	LIÈGE 7
ABBEVILLE 14	LENS 11		VALENCIENNES 12	NAMUR 8	MARCHE 9
DIEPPE 16	AMIENS 17		ST QUENTIN 18	MÉZIÈRES 19	ARLON 10
	BEAUVAIS 21		SOISSONS 22		

www.ingramcontent.com/pod-product-compliance
Lightning Source LLC
Chambersburg PA
CBHW051527190426
43193CB00045BA/2372